Twayne's United States Authors Series

Sylvia E. Bowman, *Editor*

INDIANA UNIVERSITY

Jack London

Courtesy the Huntington Library

Jack London

JACK LONDON

By EARLE LABOR

Centenary College of Louisiana

(TUSAS) 230

Twayne Publishers, Inc. :: New York

In Memory

of

King Hendricks

1900–1970

ABOUT THE AUTHOR

Earle Labor, an authority on Jack London, was invited by King Hendricks to serve as guest professor at Utah State University in 1966. He taught the first course on London ever offered by an American university; as Fulbright lecturer at Aarhus University, Denmark, in 1973, he presented the first course on London in Western Europe. Over the past fifteen years he has published numerous articles on London and has edited *Great Short Works of Jack London* (1965, 1970). He is co-author of *A Handbook of Critical Approaches to Literature* (1966) and *Mandala: Literature for Critical Analysis* (1970). Aided by grants from the American Philosophical Society and the Huntington Library, he is presently at work with Irving Shepard preparing a definitive edition of London's early fiction and a history of the London Ranch.

Part Choctaw Indian, Dr. Labor was born in Oklahoma in 1928. He grew up in Texas and received his A.B. and M.A. degrees fom Southern Methodist University, where he was a member of Phi Beta Kappa and a champion weightlifter. After serving as a recruit instructor in the U.S. Navy, in 1955 he began teaching at Centenary College in Louisiana, where he is currently professor of American literature. He received his Ph.D. from the University of Wisconsin in 1961. From 1962 to 1966 he served as Chairman of the Humanities Division at Adrian College, and in the summer of 1971 was a participant in the Harvard Visiting Faculty Program.

Preface

"Critics who turn partisan and exaggerate the worth of their subject," Max Westbrook warns us, "commit a deceptive condescension and insult both themselves and their 'man.'"[1] This caveat has been very much in my thoughts as I have put the finishing touches on the present study. I realize that my twenty years' association with Jack London has turned me partisan—to be otherwise under the circumstances would require a clinical detachment I neither possess nor desire. Even while recognizing this partisanship, I earnestly believe I have not exaggerated the worth of my subject; I think, if anything, I have underestimated that worth. For very lately the realization has come to me that the full magnitude of London's achievement persists in eluding us. My great hope is that the coming critical generation will have the understanding and the resources to assess him justly and fully.

That assessment must begin with the recognition of Jack London as a major figure in American literature. The published facts, aside from any critical interpretation, will permit no other conclusion. London was the most flamboyant literary representative of the Strenuous Age in America. At the height of that era his name was a byword for rugged individualism and romantic adventure, and his private life was front-page copy for every major newspaper in the country.[2] In the decade preceding World War I, London dominated the public imagination —and the literary marketplace—as few authors have done, before or since. His fabulous career meshed with the Golden Era of the Magazine (his success was, in large measure, predicated on the popularity of the magazine), and he commanded top dollar in the best: the *Atlantic, Century, Harper's, Collier's, Cosmopolitan, Saturday Evening Post.* Virtually everything he wrote, he sold—and he wrote a thousand words a day for seventeen years. During the years from 1900 until his death in 1916, he produced over fifty books with an astonishing range of subjects: agronomy, architecture, astral projection, boating, ecology, gold-hunting, hoboing, loving, penal reform, prize-fighting, Socialism, warfare. He became one of the world's most translated, most widely read authors.[3] Today, persistent neglect by the academic critics notwithstanding, more than eighty editions of his works are listed in *Books in Print*.

Because of the scope of London's work, I must in this brief introduction be suggestive rather than exhaustive. My aim is to provide the reader with a reasonably accurate guide to the literary world of Jack London, much of which has remained a dark continent for the critics. Most are vaguely aware of *The Sea-Wolf* and of a handful of the Klondike stories because these may still be encountered in junior high school anthologies and in the old "B" movies on the TV late shows. But few realize that London pioneered in the apocalyptic novel and dystopian fiction, that a major segment of his work deals with the American Dream and the Myth of Success, that parts of his *People of the Abyss* compare favorably with William Blake's treatises on the poor of industrial England, that his indictments of the white man's exploitation of the South Seas are as incisive as Herman Melville's, and that his fictional use of Freud and Jung anticipated the new literature of the 1920's. Most of the critics do not know these things because they have not read him.

While it is impossible to deal individually with London's more than five hundred separately published items within the limits of this book, I do indicate the extent of the London canon and have selected for specific analysis works that represent his major thematic concerns as well as his distinctive stylistic and temperamental characteristics. In providing this representative treatment, I have reluctantly omitted discussions of some of his finest stories: "Love of Life" and "The Law of Life" (two of his most unforgettable Northland tales), "The League of Old Men" (his own personal favorite), "Lost Face" and " 'Just Meat' " (frightening tales of sadism and greed), "All Gold Canyon" (a poetic dramatization of the rape of the wilderness), "The Chinago" (a brilliant satire on the White Man's Burden), "Told in the Drooling Ward" (a subtly comic parable about the "normal" and the "feeble-minded"), "The Mexican" and "A Piece of Steak" (classics of the Ring), "The Night-Born" and "Samuel" (extraordinary portrayals of the Great Mother archetype), and "War" (a little masterpiece which deserves to be ranked with the best war stories of Stephen Crane and Ernest Hemingway). I can only hope that more readers will be encouraged to discover these treasures for themselves.

In addition to pointing out the extent of London's work, I also attempt to probe the mystery of his remarkable creative genius. On one level the animation of that genius was the direct result of the dynamics of his cultural mythology: Jack London was a self-made man who drove himself to spectacular heights because his social conscience whispered that in America "getting ahead" was not merely possible but expected. In other words, he was motivated by the same cultural imperative that has driven the American hero ever since Benjamin Franklin demonstrated that the Puritan work ethic could be pleasurable as well as profitable. Success, in its peculiar American version, is a key factor in London's career; and because of his overwhelming commitment to the American Dream, much of what he wrote speaks forcefully to our own era.

But the tension produced by the individual ego working to assert its mastery over the phenomenal world is not the deepest source of London's creative energy. That source is deeper than the American culture, and to give it a label I must resort to Carl Jung, who used such terms as "the collective unconscious" and "primordial vision." As I suggest in analyzing several of London's works, not only was he a dedicated professional craftsman, but he often wrote better than he knew. Ironically, though he considered himself supremely rational—a scientific thinker and a "materialistic monist"—his most enduring work was generated from psychological depths beyond his logical understanding. *The Call of the Wild* is an outstanding case in point, but it is only one of many such instances. We cannot fully comprehend London's artistic significance until we have plumbed those psychic depths.

When I say that Jack London merits recognition as a "major figure" in American literature, I use the term advisedly. His status as a great writer or as a major American author is yet to be established. I am personally convinced he deserves serious consideration for both offices, but I can not confer such honors— they must be won by fair election at the critical polls. My primary aim is to place London's name on the ballot.

EARLE LABOR

Centenary College of Louisiana

Acknowledgments

This study represents a project so extended in its duration that I can justify it to myself only in the belief that it is a lifetime undertaking. It began a quarter century ago when my friend P. B. Lindsey, studying the American novel under Professor George Bond at Southern Methodist University, introduced me to *Martin Eden.* "It's a very powerful book, Earle," he told me; "you've got to read it." As has been the case with countless young people, that agonizing story of intellectual awakening and disenchantment, vitally rendered from the author's own struggle to rise in the world, affected me profoundly—so profoundly that I decided to make Jack London "the man" for my scholarly research. With the help of A. P. Palmer of Carol's Book Shop in Shreveport, I began collecting London books, many of which were out of print; then, under the sympathetic direction of Harry Hayden Clark of the University of Wisconsin, I completed my doctoral requirements by writing a dissertation on Jack London's literary artistry.

During the ensuing years my concern to produce some kind of useful critical work on London has been periodically revived and my scholarly morale has been sustained by such friends as Sam Baskett, Steve Dhondt, Lilian Furst, Wilfred Guerin, Howard L. Lachtman, Lee Morgan, Diane Price, James Sisson, Dick Weiderman, and John Willingham—their generous encouragement has meant more to me than I can ever tell. Over the same decade were published materials which I have used, in modified form, in this book. I should like to express my gratitude for the permission to draw freely from my previous publications: to Hensley C. Woodbridge, editor of the *Jack London Newsletter,* for several essays printed in that journal; to Harwood P. Hinton, editor of *Arizona and the West,* for my "Dedication to the Memory of Jack London, 1876–1916" (VI, 2 [Summer, 1964], 92–96); to G. B. Tennyson, editor of *Nineteenth-Century Fiction,* and Mrs. Harrietta Buford of the University of California Press, for "Jack London's Symbolic Wilderness:

Four Versions," *Nineteenth-Century Fiction* (XVII, 2 [September, 1972], 149–61); to Rochelle Girson and Roberta Craig of *Saturday Review*, for my reviews of *Stories of Hawaii by Jack London* (April 3, 1965, pp. 43–44) and *Letters from Jack London* (September 25, 1965, pp. 38–39); to Frank L. Hoskins, Jr., editor of *Studies in Short Fiction*, for "Jack London's Twice Told Tale" (IV [Summer, 1967], 334–47); and to Elisabeth Jakab, editor of the Harper Perennial Library, for my Introduction to *Great Short Works of Jack London* (New York, 1965, 1970).

Also I wish to acknowledge my indebtedness to President John Harper Dawson of Adrian College for the summer grant which in 1963 helped me translate my dissertation into something fairly readable; to Dean T. N. Marsh and the Faculty Research Awards Committee of Centenary College for the two Hemenway Grants which enabled me to make this work into something publishable; and to Ruby George and Irene Winterrowd for helping type the manuscript. I owe many thanks to Tony Bubka, Russ Kingman, Sal Noto, and James Sisson for their generosity in checking the manuscript in its entirety; its present accuracy is due in large measure to their discerning eyes—any inaccuracies are due to my own faulty vision.

I am deeply indebted to Irving Shepard, executor of the London Estate, who has not only permitted me to quote from London's writings in this book, but who has through his friendship given me new insight into, and new interest in, London's work. I wish to express my appreciation at the same time to Dr. James Thorpe and the Henry E. Huntington Library Committee on Fellowships for the grants provided for my research in 1972 and 1973; to Mary Isabel Fry and the Huntington Library Staff for their gracious assistance during my visits to the library; and to Jean Preston and Robert O. Dougan for permission to use materials from the Jack London Collection in this book. I am also grateful to Dr. Milton C. Abrams and A. J. Simmonds of Utah State University for permitting me to use the London materials in the Merrill Library.

I owe most of all to King Hendricks, who by personal example reinforced my trust in the essential nobility of man as well as my faith in Jack London. And, of course, to Betty Labor, who has helped me put it all together.

Contents

Preface

Acknowledgments

Chronology

1. The American Adam   17

2. The Literary Frontiersman   40

3. Success   82

4. The Symbolic Wilderness   124

5. A Man for Almost All Literary Seasons   147

    Notes and References   151

    Selected Bibliography   165

    Index   173

Chronology

1876   Jack London born in San Francisco, California, January 12, the only child of Flora Wellman, who named as the father William Henry Chaney, an itinerant astrologer she had lived with during the years 1874-75. On September 7, 1876, she married John London, a widower with two daughters, Eliza and Ida. The baby was named John Griffith London.

1891   After living on several farms and ranches in California, London completed grammar school in Oakland. Worked in cannery. Purchased sloop, the *Razzle-Dazzle*, with $300 loaned by "Mammy Jenny" Prentiss. Raided oyster beds; then joined the California Fish Patrol.

1893   Seven-month voyage aboard the sealing schooner *Sophia Sutherland*. Won first prize in contest for "best descriptive article" in San Francisco *Morning Call* for "Story of a Typhoon off the Coast of Japan."

1894   Tramping experiences, later recounted in *The Road* (1907).

1895   Finished public-school education at Oakland High School where he wrote sketches for student magazine, *The High School Aegis*.

1896   Joined Socialist Labor Party. Attended the University of California for one semester.

1897   Joined Klondike gold rush and spent winter in the Yukon. Death of John London.

1898   Returned from the Yukon and undertook writing as a profession.

1899   Published "To the Man on Trail" and other Northland stories in the *Overland Monthly*; began selling other items to magazines and newspapers.

1900   Published "An Odyssey of the North" in the *Atlantic Monthly*. Married Bessie Maddern. *The Son of the Wolf* published.

1901   First daughter, Joan, born, January 15.

1902   Lived for six weeks in East End of London, England, collecting materials for *The People of the Abyss* (1903). Second daughter, Becky, born, October 20. First novel, *A Daughter of the Snows*, published by J. B. Lippincott.

1903   Separated from Bessie. *The Call of the Wild* brought him world-wide acclaim.

1904 Hearst correspondent for Russo-Japanese War. Divorce proceedings initiated by Bessie.
1905 Married Charmian Kittredge. Purchased ranch near Glen Ellen, California. Lectured throughout East, including stop at Harvard.
1906 Lectured at Yale, Carnegie Hall, and throughout Midwest. Reported San Francisco earthquake for *Collier's*. Began building famous sailboat, the *Snark*.
1907 Sailed from Oakland on the *Snark*; visited Hawaii, the Marquesas, and Tahiti. Publicly accused of "nature faking" by President Theodore Roosevelt.
1908 After brief return home aboard the steamship *Mariposa* to straighten out financial affairs, continued *Snark* voyage: to Samoa, the Fijis, New Hebrides, and the Solomons. Answered President Roosevelt's nature-faking charge in article "The Other Animals" (*Collier's*, September 5).
1909 Hospitalized in Sydney, Australia, with multiple tropical ailments. Abandoned plans for sailing *Snark* around the world; returned home via Ecuador, Panama, New Orleans, and Grand Canyon.
1910 Devoted energies to building "Beauty Ranch"; started construction of Wolf House, mansion designed to stand "a thousand years." Birth and death of daughter Joy.
1911 Drove four-horse carriage with Charmian and manservant Nakata through Northern California and Oregon.
1912 Sailed around Cape Horn aboard the *Dirigo*. Charmian's second baby lost (miscarriage).
1913 Published *The Abysmal Brute*, prize-fight novel based on "The Dress-Suit Pugilist," one of several plots purchased from Sinclair Lewis; and *John Barleycorn*, best-selling autobiographical treatise on alcoholism. Wolf House destroyed by fire, presumably arson.
1914 Reported Mexican Revolution for *Collier's*; forced to return home by severe case of dysentery.
1915 Spent several months in Hawaii, hoping to improve health.
1916 Resigned from Socialist Party "because of its lack of fire and fight, and its loss of emphasis on the class struggle." Suffered severe bouts of uremia and rheumatism; warned by his doctors to restrict drinking and diet. Died November 22; bulletin issued by four attending physicians attributed cause of death to "gastro-intestinal type of uraemia."

CHAPTER 1

The American Adam

N O great American idol," the historian Dixon Wecter tells us, "has lacked a touch lent by the struggle against odds, or by discouragement and passing failure. He must be a man who fights uphill."[1] Wecter's comment is most useful in helping us to understand the phenomenal career of Jack London, a literary idol who became a national legend before he reached the age of thirty.[2] No major figure in American literature struggled against greater odds, none fought uphill with more spectacular success, and none achieved wider popularity. He was born out of wedlock, reared under the constant threat of hardship, spent much of his adolescence in delinquency, and entered maturity without formal professional training—yet he succeeded in becoming one of the most widely read, most highly paid authors of his epoch. In reviewing the facts of his life, we can readily appreciate the observation that "the greatest story Jack London ever wrote was the story he lived."[3]

Even in America that story seems incredible. As late as his own twenty-third year London might have echoed the sentiments of young John Milton: "My hasting days fly on with full career,/ But my late spring no bud or blossom shew'th." He had returned penniless from the Klondike gold rush; John London had recently died, and Jack was left with the burden of supporting the family; his frantic efforts to become a professional writer had earned no more than a boxful of rejection slips. In that dark season he sent a pathetic letter to his sweetheart: "Forgive my not writing," he began, "for I have been miserable and half sick. So nervous this morning that I could hardly shave myself. . . . Everything seems to have gone wrong— why, I haven't received my twenty dollars from those essays

17

yet. Not a word as to how I stood in my Civil Exs. Not a word
from the *Youth's Companion*, and it means to me what no one
can possibly realize."[4]

But from this adversity came the kind of vital resolution that
characterized Jack London throughout his life. "I don't care if
the whole present, all I possess, were swept away from me,"
he declared in another letter to her three days afterwards, "I
will build a new present; if I am left naked and hungry to-
morrow—before I give in I will go on naked and hungry; if I were
a woman I would prostitute myself to all men but that I would
succeed—in short, I will" (*Letters from Jack London*, 7–8).

And, in short, he did. His resolution was prophetic. Within a
year he had overwhelmed the "bitch-goddess SUCCESS" (as William James called our national obsession) by muscling his way
into the exclusive pages of the *Atlantic Monthly* and by signing
his first book contract with a distinguished Boston publishing
house. Within five years his sociological crusades and his personal
escapades, counterpointing his Northland adventure tales, made
his name international newscopy. During the eighteen years
from his resolution in 1898 until his death in 1916 he accomplished enough to satisfy a half-dozen normally ambitious men.
He managed to support several families from his earnings as a
writer. He traveled, lectured, and wrote freely in behalf of the
Socialist Party. He risked his life by disappearing into the hell-
holes of London's East End to gather firsthand material for an
impressive sociological report, *The People of the Abyss*. He
worked as a war correspondent during the Russo-Japanese War
of 1904 and the Mexican Revolution of 1914. Moreover, his newspaper articles on professional boxing signalized a new field of
sports writing. He built and sailed his own ship, the fabled *Snark*,
halfway around the globe. He became a landowner and country
gentleman, developing in Northern California's Valley of the
Moon a magnificent estate, part of which is now the Jack London State Historic Park. A friend to horticulturist Luther Burbank, London pioneered in modern agricultural methods and
livestock breeding. He worked hard to bring about reforms in
the California penal system, giving free room and board to
paroled convicts at his ranch. An eclectic reader, he responded
not only to the work of such established literary figures as

Robert Louis Stevenson, Rudyard Kipling, and Joseph Conrad, but also to the radical new extraliterary concepts of Sigmund Freud and Carl Jung. At the same time he managed somehow to answer countless letters from friends, aspiring writers, down-and-outers, literary admirers, editors, and curiosity-mongers. In this same eighteen-year period, London also produced a half-hundred books.

I *The Mythic Hero*

The hero is he whom every American should wish to be. His legend is the mirror of the folk soul.   —Dixon Wecter

Born only fourteen years before the 1890 census marked the closing of the frontier, coming of age during that decade called "the watershed of American history,"[5] and dying less than a year before the United States entered World War I, London personified the most crucial transition in this nation's cultural development. Although America's childhood had been left behind at Gettysburg and Appomattox, America's maturity was delayed; it was still the Age of Adolescence, with the manifestations of tension, instability, extravagance, and contrariness which characterize this phase in nations as well as in individuals. Jack London's generation was the last fully possessed of that "coarseness and strength combined with acuteness and inquisitiveness, [that] restless nervous energy, [that] dominant individualism [and] buoyancy and exuberance" which have defined the American character as shaped by the frontier experience.[6] Aggressively optimistic, bluntly honest but unselfconscious, dynamic, and extraverted, London was himself a child of that experience. Yet he became a man of the twentieth century: complex, hypersensitive, fragmented, melancholic—at moments self-destructive and aware of the darkness within the human heart.[7]

His nature was as contradictory and his moods as extreme as those of another legendary folk writer whose meteor overlapped London's: Mark Twain. Both men were paradoxical figures shaped by their frontier heritage as well as by the transitions of the late nineteenth century. Franklin Walker has indicated this heritage as a key to London's life and work,[8]

and Howard Mumford Jones's explanation of the frontier paradox—though intended for Twain—describes London just as
aptly: "If we lump together all the inconsistent definitions of
the frontier common in American history, if we seek any thread
running through the kaleidoscopic aspects of a society emerging
from the wilderness with astonishing rapidity, what can we say?
Is not the common element *incongruity*—that juxtaposition of
the new and the old, of the traditional and the unexpected, of
cherished memories out of the past and an inability now to understand the inner life that produced the phenomena?"[9]

This conglomerate of apparent inconsistencies has made Jack
London a difficult subject for scholarly analysis. He insisted,
especially in his later years, that he hated writing and that he
wrote only for money; but most of his work departed sharply
from the best-seller formulas of his age, and he was militant
in defending his literary sincerity. On the one hand, he was
dedicated to telling the truth as he saw it; on the other, he
could not resist a penchant for bardic exaggeration. Despite
his reputation as a crude, red-blooded Naturalist, his fictional
treatment of sex was embarrassingly genteel. Honest to a fault
in his personal relationships, he was a sharp horse trader who
was capable of swapping his worst hack writing for hard cash.
Big-hearted, generous to the verge of bankruptcy, he also had a
remarkable talent for petty squabbling and invective. A humani-
tarian with profound compassion for the underdog, regardless
of color or class, he nevertheless believed in the supremacy of the
Anglo-Saxon race.

A tough fighter, relentless when his ego was challenged, he
was a warmly sensitive friend and a sentimental lover. He was
the manliest of men, yet he never outgrew his weaknesses for
childish fun and games, practical jokes, and candy. Despite his
love of the outdoors and his reputation as a superman, his
medical history is an appalling record of debilitating ailments;
and, physically, he was worn-out by the age of forty. Self-
educated, he considered himself a great thinker, yet he could
unblinkingly accommodate to his *weltanschauung* the disparate
philosophical attitudes of Friedrich Nietzsche, Karl Marx, Ernst
Haeckel, Herbert Spencer, and Benjamin Kidd,[10] while blandly
admitting that metaphysicians like Ralph Waldo Emerson and

Henri Bergson were beyond him. A rugged individualist who preached Socialism, London fought his crusade for World Revolution with a unique mixture of Marxist piety and frontier pep. While he insisted he was a logical positivist and a materialistic monist, his best work is permeated by poetry and myth. If this image of Jack London confuses us, we should bear in mind that, in the first place, many of these apparent discrepancies were the manifestations of a dynamic personality and a versatile intelligence—and that, furthermore, viewed from the frontier perspective, Jack London was no more paradoxical than the American character itself. His life-style was a symbolic epitome of the greater myth, and not even Walt Whitman, who devoted all his genius to projecting this archetype, could so thoroughly incarnate in his personal identity the traits of the American folk hero.

II *The Hero as Juvenile*

In *The American Adam,* R. W. B. Lewis has defined this mythic figure as "a radically new personality, the hero of the new adventure: an individual emancipated from history, happily bereft of ancestry, untouched and undefiled by the usual inheritances of family and race; an individual standing alone, self-reliant and self-propelling, ready to confront whatever awaited him with the aid of his own unique and inherent resources."[11] The definition might have been tailored to suit Jack London, who was born in the poorer district of San Francisco, a "natural" child, literally if not happily bereft of ancestry; for his paternity has never been conclusively established. Several biographers, including London's own daughter Joan, have suggested that the father was William Henry Chaney, a footloose astrologer with whom Flora Wellman, his mother, had lived in 1875;[12] it was Chaney whom Flora named as father on the infant's birth certificate. But Chaney had left her in an indignant rage when he learned of her pregnancy; and when, many years afterwards, Jack wrote to Chaney asking him if he were truly his father, the old man insisted that he had been impotent at the time of the child's conception and could not possibly have been the father. In any case, eight months after the child's birth, Flora Wellman

Chaney married John London, a widower who had two daughters and who treated the boy as his own from that time forward. Aside from the question of Jack's paternal ancestry, it is clear that he felt the threat of poverty during his early years. John London was a good father and a conscientious worker, but his vitalities had been sapped by Civil War injuries and by chronic misfortune. The get-rich schemes and the frequent moves instigated by Flora aggravated the family's economic problems. At an early age Jack was forced by necessity to become a self-propelling individualist confronting circumstance and destiny "with the aid of his own unique and inherent resources." Describing his childhood miseries in a letter to Mabel Applegarth, he wrote:

... I have fought and am fighting my battle alone. . . . Do you know my childhood? When I was seven years old, at the country school of San Pedro, this happened. Meat, I was that hungry for it I once opened a girl's basket and stole a piece of meat—a little piece the size of my two fingers. . . . In those days, like Esau, I would have literally sold my birthright for a mess of pottage, a piece of meat. . . . This meat incident is a epitome of my whole life. I was eight years old when I put on my first undershirt made at or bought at a store. Duty—at ten years I was on the streets selling newspapers. Every cent was turned over to my people, and I went to school in constant shame of the hats, shoes, clothes I wore. Duty—from then on I had no childhood. Up at three o'clock in the morning to carry papers. When that was finished I did not go home but continued on to school. School out, my evening papers. Saturday I worked on an ice wagon. Sunday I went to a bowling alley and set up pins for drunken Dutchmen. Duty—I turned over every cent and went dressed like a scarecrow.   (*Letters from Jack London*, 5–6)

Later, in a letter to his first publisher, he asserted, ". . . from my ninth year, with the exception of the hours spent at school (and I earned them by hard labor), my life has been one of toil" (*Letters*, 86). But, lest it seem that he was nothing more than a drudge—"a work beast," as he called himself—it should be pointed out he was able repeatedly to escape the dull routine of toil.

His first means of escape was through romantic literature. "I always could read and write," he boasted, "and have no recollection antedating such a condition. Folks say I simply insisted upon being taught. Was an omnivorous reader. . . . Remember reading some of Trowbridge's works for boys at six years of age. At seven I was reading Paul du Chaillu's *Travels*, Captain Cook's *Voyages*, and *Life of Garfield*. . . . At eight I was deep in Ouida and Washington Irving" (*Letters*, 86). For those familiar only with the Jack London legend and not with the boy behind the legend it comes as something of a shock to realize that as a youngster he was regarded by his grade school classmates as a "bookworm." At the age of eleven, after his family had moved back to the city after five years of living on farms and ranches, Jack discovered the Oakland Public Library, a major event in his life. "It was this world of books, now accessible, that practically gave me the basis of my education," he later explained: "Not until I began fighting for a living and making my first successes so that I was able to buy books for myself did I ever discontinue drawing many books on many library cards from out of the Oakland free public library" (*Letters*, 439).

So desperately did London crave the riches he found in this new world that for weeks he haunted the library, spending every spare hour with its treasures. Years afterwards he recalled with some humor that he had very nearly developed a case of St. Vitus dance in his hollow-eyed nervous exhaustion: "I read mornings, afternoons, and nights. I read in bed, read at table, I read as I walked to and from school, and I read at recess while the other boys were playing."[13]

But such bibliomania could not last. Hard work brought him back into the real world. Shortly after finishing grade school, he went to work full-time in Hickmott's cannery in West Oakland, where the working day ranged from ten to twenty hours. A traumatic experience, the cannery ordeal indelibly impressed upon young Jack the deadly odium of physical toil. His later story "The Apostate" was emotionally, if not literally, autobiographical; of "Johnny," the boy in the story, London wrote: "There was no joyousness in life for him. The procession of the days he never saw. The nights he slept away in twitching unconsciousness. . . . He had no mental life whatever; yet deep down in the crypts of his mind, unknown to him, were being

weighed and sifted every hour of his toil, every movement of
his hands, every twitch of his muscles, and preparations were
making for a future course of action that would amaze him and
all his little world."[14]

Johnny, the apostate, deserts his role as a "work-beast" by
suddenly hopping a freight train. In similar spirit Jack borrowed
three hundred dollars from his onetime wet nurse "Mammy
Jenny" Prentiss, bought a sloop, joined the hoodlum gang on
the Oakland waterfront, and became at the age of fifteen "Prince
of the Oyster Pirates." "San Francisco Bay is no mill pond by
the way," he wrote about those irresponsible years; "I was a
salmon fisher, an oyster pirate, a schooner sailor, a fish patrol-
man, a longshoreman, and a general sort of bay-faring adven-
turer—a boy in years and a man amongst men." Yet even during
these adventures he did not lose his craving for books: "Always
a book, and always reading when the rest were asleep; when
they were awake I was one with them, for I was always a good
comrade" (*Letters*, 86). The American Adam, no matter how
keen his intellectual appetite, never allowed books to preempt
manly comradeship.

Reminiscing about his juvenile escapades, London remarked
that all his waterfront colleagues had wound up either dead
or behind bars; and perhaps the greatest miracle of his miracu-
lous career was that he managed to reach manhood at all, for
he was a habitual friend to danger as well as to his fellow man.
The mettle he displayed in those adventures reminds us time
and again of another famous boy-hero: Huck Finn. Like Huck,
Jack—or the "Frisco Kid," as he dubs his alter ego in *The Cruise
of the Dazzler*—was a self-made youth who possessed the quick-
ness of wit and body, the insouciant courage, the agility and
toughness we so admire in our heroes, be they athletes or
astronauts. And, of course, he was the gritty Bad Boy whom
we have shamelessly idolized, whether in the mischievous characters of Huck and Tom, Penrod and Sam, and Dennis the
Menace—or in the more sinister forms of Billy the Kid, "Pretty
Boy" Floyd, and Clyde Barrow.

The frequency with which these adventures of London's youth
are used in his writings suggests that he himself saw in them
more than commercial fodder; they represented the Eden of

carefree boyhood to which we all periodically return in our daydreams. He devoted two entire books—*The Cruise of the Dazzler* and *Tales of the Fish Patrol*—and parts of a half-dozen others to fictionalized projections of this juvenile persona. In *The Valley of the Moon*, for instance, the heroine, during a stroll along the Bay shore, makes the acquaintance of a thirteen-year-old boy named John who tells her his dreams of glory:

"Don't you sometimes feel you'd die if you didn't know what's beyond them hills an' what's beyond the other hills behind them hills? An' the Golden Gate! There's the Pacific Ocean beyond, and China an' Japan, an' India, an' . . . an' all the coral islands. You can go any-where out through the Golden Gate—to Australia, to Africa, to the seal islands, to the North Pole, to Cape Horn. Why, all them places are just waitin' for me to come an' see 'em. I've lived in Oakland all my life, but I'm not going to live in Oakland the rest of my life, not by a long shot. I'm goin' to get away . . . away. . . ."[15]

London was undoubtedly recalling the far music of his own youthful dreams. Within a week of his seventeenth birthday, jaded with his bay-faring life, he shipped before the mast as an able seaman on the *Sophia Sutherland*, a sealing schooner bound for Japan and the Bering Sea.

III *The Wonderful Boy—Manqué*

The seven-month voyage aboard the "*Sophie*" *Sutherland*, as Jack called her, was relatively unspectacular, but it yielded several important results, including materials that London would profitably use later. Most immediately, it provided evidence that, with a bit of touching up, the stuff of raw experience could be exchanged for cash. Two months after his ship had docked, the San Francisco *Morning Call* sponsored a creative-writing contest for young talent. Encouraged by his mother, Jack wrote a brief narrative sketch that described a typhoon he had experienced during his voyage. Simply titled "Story of a Typhoon off the Coast of Japan," the piece was an unusual accomplish-ment for a seventeen-year-old youth with only a grade-school education. Fresh, vivid, unpretentious, it still reads well. It reveals, moreover, several of the characteristics which distinguish London's mature work: a natural feel for graceful syntax and for imagery that evokes multiple sensory response, particularly through sound-symbolism—

. . . Huge gunies rose slowly, fluttering their wings in the light breeze and striking their webbed feet on the surface of the water for over half a mile before they could leave it. Hardly had the patter, patter died away when a flock of sea quail rose, and with whistling wings flew away to windward, where members of a large band of whales were disporting themselves, their blowings sounding like the exhaust of steam engines. The harsh, discordant cries of a sea-parrot grated unpleasantly on the ear, and set half a dozen on the alert in a small band of seals that were ahead of us. Away they went, breaching and jumping entirely out of the water. A seagull with slow, deliberate flight and long majestic curves, circled round us, and as a reminder of home a little English sparrow perched impudently on the fo'castle head, and cocking his head on one side chirped merrily. The boats were soon among the seals, and the bang! bang! of the guns could be heard from down to leeward.[16]

The story contains more than good descriptive detail. Added to the narrative suspense as the ship suffers the rising violence of the great storm, and synchronized with it, is the dying agony of one of the crew-members, an ex-bricklayer who has tuberculosis. London's conclusion shows the natural instinct of the story-teller to correlate natural phenomenon and human interest: "And so with the storm passed away 'the bricklayer's' soul." Amateur work, obviously, it nevertheless hints of a genuine talent which also impressed the judges of the *Morning Call* contest. They awarded Jack the twenty-five-dollar first prize over second- and third-place entries by college students from Berkeley and Stanford.

With a bit of luck Jack London might have developed then and there into another Thomas Chatterton, the Wonderful Boy. Elated by his victory, he whipped out a half-dozen more short pieces. But the contest was past, and though he had received money for writing, he was still a long way from being a professional.

IV   *The Wonderful Year—Manqué*

Indeed, it seemed to him as though, this year, education went mad.
. . . Chicago asked in 1893 for the first time the question whether
the American people knew where they were driving.
—Henry Adams, *The Education of Henry Adams*

Eighteen ninety-three was the *annus mirabilis* of the 1890's.
This was the year in which a young professor from the
University of Wisconsin delivered a paper at the annual conven-
tion of the American Historical Society which not only earned
him tenure but also established a new field of historiography.
"American social development has been continually beginning
over again on the frontier," the paper read. "This perennial
rebirth, this fluidity of American life, this expansion westward
with its new opportunities, its continuous touch with the
simplicity of primitive society, furnish the forces dominating
American character. . . . And now, four centuries from the discovery of America, at the end of a hundred years of life under
the Constitution, the frontier has gone, and with its going has
closed the first period of American history."

The speaker was Frederick Jackson Turner, and his statement
contains the essence of the now-famous "Turner Thesis": The
frontier had vanished, and vanished with it was the Edenic
dream. "Since the days when the fleet of Columbus sailed into
the waters of the New World, America has been another name
for opportunity, and the people of the United States have taken
their tone from the incessant expansion which has not only
been open but has even been forced upon them. . . . But never
again will such gifts of free land offer themselves" (*Turner
Thesis,* 18). If there was a touch of nostalgia in Turner's pro-
nouncement, such was the only proper attitude for the late nineteenth-century intellectual historian. Henry Adams, the brilliant
self-proclaimed pariah of the country's most distinguished family,
also felt it strongly and observed that "during this last decade
everyone talked, and seemed to feel *fin-de-siècle.*"[17] Civilization
had come to a crossroads, and America had already chosen its
new path.

Eighteen ninety-three was also the year of the great Columbian
Exposition in Chicago, and what Henry Adams saw there was

a clear if unsettling indication of the new way. "Education ran riot at Chicago," he wrote in his prophetic autobiography. The alleged unity of natural force which had for ages anchored the logical faith of the historian was at Chicago unmasked as fond delusion; and the historical mind, hitherto attuned to metaphysical and political causality, was helpless when confronted with mechanical sequence. The ultimate destiny for an America bound to such sequence might be in grave question, but the direction itself was unmistakable: "For a hundred years . . . the American people had hesitated, vacillated. swayed forward and back, between two forces, one simply industrial, the other capitalistic, centralizing, and mechanical. In 1893, the issue came on the single gold standard, and the majority at last declared itself, once for all, in favor of the capitalistic system with all its necessary machinery" (*The Education of Henry Adams*, 344).

Parts for this necessary machinery were an overseas market for manufactured goods and a huge labor force—preferably with a surplus of laborers—to produce those goods. America found herself in possession of these and the other necessary parts by the end of the nineteenth century. Unfortunately among the risks of capitalism was that of severe economic recession, and overseas interests enhanced that risk. Eighteen ninety-three was, in consequence, the year of the economic catastrophe known as the Great Panic; and it ushered in what Samuel Eliot Morison and Henry Steele Commager have described as the darkest period in American history since the Civil War.[18] To save the nation, Jacob Coxey, a wealthy quarry owner in Massillon, Ohio, decided that he would lead an army of unemployed workers in protest to the steps of the Capitol in Washington, D.C.

While "General" Coxey was formulating his strategy, Jack London was busily learning the facts about the new American system as an industrial buck private. His first job after returning from sea had been in the jute mills, where he worked for the same wages that he had received years earlier as a boy-worker in the cannery. Deciding that he must learn a trade, he presented himself eagerly to the superintendent at the power plant for the Oakland Street Railway to whom he offered his muscle-power cheaply in return for a chance to become an electrician: ". . . I still believed in the old myths which were the heritage of the American boy when I was a boy. A canal boy could become a President. Any boy, who took employment with any firm, could, by thrift, energy and sobriety, learn the business and rise from position to position until he was taken in as a junior partner. After that the senior partnership was only a matter of time. Very often—so ran the myth—the boy, by reason of his steadiness and application, married his employer's daughter" (*John Barleycorn*, 187-88).

Jack was indeed "taken in," but not in the sense he anticipated, and his reward was not the boss's daughter—it was a two-man job at less than half pay: the alert superintendent, with his eye on the main chance, hired the eager youth at thirty dollars a month to replace two coal-shovelers at forty dollars each. Instead of making an electrician out of him, London recollected, that superintendent had decided to make fifty dollars a month out of him. For several weeks London endured an orgy of work the like of which he had never imagined, even in the cannery and jute mills; but he was finally rescued by one of the older hands at the plant who risked his own job to tell Jack about the superintendent's shenanigan. "Learning a trade could go hang," London decided when he learned the ruse. "It was a whole lot better to royster and frolic over the world in the way I had previously done. So I headed out on the adventure-path again, starting to tramp East by beating my way on the railroads" (*John Barleycorn*, 201). At this point his personal destiny meshed with the larger economic forces set in motion during the Critical Year.

V *Portrait of the Artist as a Road-Kid*

... I became a tramp—well, because of the life that was in me, of the wanderlust in my blood that would not let me rest. ... I went on "The Road" because I couldn't keep away from it; because I hadn't the price of the railroad fare in my jeans; because I was so made that I couldn't work all my life on "one same shift"; because— well, just because it was easier to than not to. ... The Road had gripped me and would not let me go; and later, when I had voyaged to the sea and done one thing and another, I returned to The Road to make longer flights, to be a "comet" and a profesh, and to plump into the bath of sociology that wet me to the skin.

—Jack London, *The Road*

If the sea had served as Jack London's Harvard, "The Road"—
and by this he meant the railroad—was his Yale. As early as his
oyster-pirating days, he had lucked into "a push" of road-kids
who taught him how to ride the "blinds" over "the hill" (the
Sierra Nevada), how to "batter the main stem for light pieces"
(to beg for money on the main street), and how to "throw his
feet" for hand-outs. Consequently, the announcement in the
Oakland newspapers that "General" Charles T. Kelly would lead
the Western contingent of Coxey's Army of the Unemployed
across the nation on flatcars was all the excuse Jack needed to
hit The Road again.

And the march to Washington was nothing more than an
excuse; at this stage, he was interested in adventure, not in
sociology. "Sociology was merely incidental," he admitted;
"it came afterward, in the same manner that a wet skin follows
a ducking."[19] He spent no more than a month with Kelly's Army,
missing its departure on the morning of April 6, 1894; catching
up with it in Council Bluffs, Iowa; "hustling chewin's" down
the Des Moines River; finally deserting the army and head-
ing out on his own near the end of May from Sam Clemens's
home town, Hannibal, Missouri. London wanted to tour the
country and see the World's Fair at Chicago, a much finer
prospect than getting arrested for trespassing on the Capitol
lawn—the May Day anticlimax for Coxey's dream of reform.

Jack saw the Fair, but he was too naive to see the deeper
significances that had worried Henry Adams. London's own
philosophical awakening would start abruptly a month later
near Niagara Falls. En route, he spent several days at the home
of his Aunt Mary Everhard in St. Joseph, Michigan, where he
met a cousin whose name—Ernest—sounded eminently usable
for the fictionist; and a dozen years later "Ernest Everhard"
became the appropriate name of London's tough, dedicated hero
in his most famous sociological novel, *The Iron Heel*. When Jack
rode into Niagara Falls in a "side-door Pullman" (the hobo
euphemism for a box-car) on the afternoon of June 28, he went
directly to the great falls. So entranced was he that he lingered
to watch the rushing water by moonlight until eleven that
evening; then after "flopping" in a nearby field, he arose at five

the next morning to see the falls at dawn—a sight he was destined never to enjoy.

On his way he was arrested for vagrancy and sentenced without trial to thirty days in the Erie County Penitentiary. Though he had already seen much of the world's underside, he was scarcely prepared for the horrors he witnessed during the following month. "It would take a deep plummet to reach bottom in the Erie County Pen," he reflected; a deeper plummet than even the former Prince of the Oyster Pirates and Sailor Kid was willing to drop. Years later, in *The Road*, he merely skimmed the surface, excising most of the events of this experience as monstrously "unbelievable . . . unprintable . . . unthinkable" (*The Road*, 106-7).

But if these events were themselves unthinkable, they made a rugged young individualist pause for meditation about the system that fostered them. Jack had been momentarily dropped into the Pit, the "submerged tenth" of society; and it gave him a scare he would never forget. The "bath of sociology" he received in the Erie County Pen wet him deeper than the skin; it was, in fact, his philosophical baptism: "I had been reborn, but not renamed, and I was running around to find out what manner of thing I was. I ran back to California and opened the books."[20]

VI *The Books*

[His mind] had lain fallow all his life so far as the abstract thought of the books was concerned, and it was ripe for the sowing.
—Jack London, *Martin Eden*

London's half-year odyssey on The Road produced three important results. First, it sharpened his storytelling ability. "I have often thought that to this training of my tramp days is due much of my success as a story-writer," he said. "In order to get the food whereby I lived, I was compelled to tell tales that rang true. At the back door, out of inexorable necessity, is developed the convincingness and sincerity laid down by all authorities on the art of the short-story. Also, I quite believe it was my tramp-apprenticeship that made a realist out of me. Realism constitutes the only goods one can exchange at the kitchen door for grub" (*The Road*, 10). Second, it tempered his naively individualist attitude and started his questioning of the American socio-economic system: "... my joyous individualism was dominated by the orthodox bourgeois ethics. ... [But] on this new *blond-beast* adventure I found myself looking upon life from a new and totally different angle. I had dropped down from the proletariat into what sociologists love to call the 'submerged tenth,' and I was startled to discover the way in which that submerged tenth was recruited" (*War of the Classes*, 272-73).

Contrary to his previous misconception, most of the members of this fraternity of social castaways had been men as good as London himself who, by accident and hardship, had been cut loose to drift aimlessly into the hobo jungles, jails, and potters' fields. It therefore became obvious that the man who relied on his physical prowess for his livelihood did so at great peril. And this realization was the third significant result of his tramping excursion: Jack resolved to use his brain rather than his brawn to make his way in the world. This realization, as much as anything, sent him scurrying back to California to open the books.

His initial step was to resume his formal education. In January, 1895, he entered Oakland High School, a man of the world among school children. He felt foolishly out of place, but the school did provide a chance to try his hand at writing again. His school journal, *The High School Aegis*, welcomed his contributions; and, if he got no pay for his writing, he gained confidence by getting his work printed. All told, the magazine published ten of his pieces—a sociological essay, two Frisco Kid stories based on his hoboing experiences, and several sketches which show him developing his skills.

But even more significant than the education he was getting at Oakland High was what he was learning outside the school. He became an active member of the Henry Clay Debating Society where he began meeting other young intellectuals with whom he could exchange ideas and begin to articulate his growing awareness of the world of thought. He was by now reading widely, not merely books of romance, travel, and fiction, but heavier stuff: Charles Darwin's *Origin of the Species*, Adam

Smith's *The Wealth of Nations,* Immanuel Kant's *Critique of Pure Reason,* Benjamin Kidd's *Social Evolution,* and—most important—Herbert Spencer's "Philosophy of Style," to which he subsequently attributed his own mastery of style, and *First Principles,* which he claimed would do more for mankind through the ages than a thousand books like Dickens's *Nicholas Nickleby* and Harriet Beecher Stowe's *Uncle Tom's Cabin* (*Letters,* 51). Spencer's audacious synthesis of the laws of biology, physics, and sociology; his emphasis on the necessity of progress and the perfectibility of man; his survival-of-the-fittest ethic; and his advocacy of the individual over society—these were exactly what Jack's voracious intellectual appetite had been craving, and to the god who had provided them he would remain faithful for the rest of his life, long after the great Spencerian fad which swept America had declined.

There were, of course, other gods in London's pantheon. Shortly after his return from The Road, he had read *The Communist Manifesto.* From Karl Marx, Jack learned that he was no longer a rampant individualist with bourgeois ethics: without having known it, he had the makings of a Socialist. An individualist he would remain all his life—but he was no longer rampant since he recognized himself as a member of the proletariat. In April, 1896, he joined the Socialist Labor Party. Within a year he had managed to get himself arrested for soapbox oratory and to acquire notoriety as Oakland's "Boy Socialist." And for the next twenty years he signed his letters "Yours for the Revolution."

In 1896 he also decided that he did not have another two years to spend in completion of his high school education and that he could move faster on his own. He began cramming at the University Academy in Alameda. Finding the pace too slow, he began studying nineteen hours a day at home. In August he passed the entrance examinations for the University of California and began bicycling daily from Oakland to the Berkeley campus. Although he made no headlines as a college student, he did make lasting impressions on some of his fellows; James Hopper, the stocky football star who later became a member of the artists' colony at Carmel, recalled that Jack "possessed already then a certain vague reputation among us boys as one who had done many things." After they had met, Hopper discovered that, characteristically, London "was full of gigantic plans—just as, indeed, I was to find him always whenever I came upon him later in life. . . . He was going to take all the courses in English, all of them, nothing less. Also, of course, he meant to take most of the courses in the natural sciences, many in history, and bite a respectable chunk out of the philosophies."[21]

Exploiting the elective system in his status as a special student, Jack began his college career by taking three courses in English and two in history. Unfortunately, his hopes outran the pace of his professors. For one who had confronted reality firsthand, the world offered too much to waste time sitting and taking second-hand notes. Because life was so short—and funds even shorter—London withdrew from college after one semester. Disappointing though it had been, that semester had nevertheless worked as an important catalyst. "I decided immediately to embark on my career," he explained in his autobiography:

I had four preferences: first, music; second, poetry; third, the writing of philosophic, economic, and political essays; and, fourth, and last, and least, fiction writing. I resolutely cut out music as impossible, settled down in my bedroom, and tackled my second, third, and fourth choices simultaneously. Heavens, how I wrote! . . . I wrote everything—ponderous essays, scientific and sociological, short stories, humorous verse, verse of all sorts from triolets and sonnets to blank verse tragedy and elephantine epics in Spenserian stanzas. On occasion I composed steadily, day after day, for fifteen hours a day. At times I forgot to eat, or refused to tear myself away from my passionate outpouring in order to eat.   (*John Barleycorn*, pp. 220–21)

This passage is eloquent testimony to the intensity of London's dedication; the genuineness of his creative fervor belies the accusation—by himself as well as by critics—that he wrote only for money.

Without realizing it, London had virtually completed his preprofessional training by the summer of 1897; but he was not yet ready for a successful literary career. He had written too much too soon; and he later counseled other aspiring writers, "Take your time; study the stuff of the other fellows who've mastered the trick—study until you can turn the same trick. Take your time; elaborate; omit; draw; develop. Paint—paint pictures and characters and emotions—but paint [and] draw. And take your time" (*Letters,* 335). Jack himself had painted and drawn feverishly during the early months of 1897; now he needed to take time—time for taking stock, for maturing. Indeed, he was forced to take it during the coming winter.

VII   *The Long, Cold Winter*

It was in the Klondike that I found myself. There you get your perspective. I got mine.   —"JACK LONDON By Himself" (pamphlet)

Like Henry Thoreau, Jack London was born in the nick of time. Had he been three or four years later, he would have missed the last frontier stampede, which started on July 14, 1897, when the steamship *Excelsior* docked at San Francisco, disembarking forty miners who lugged a ton of gold down the gangplank. At Seattle three days later a second group carrying over two tons in gold dust and nuggets debarked from the *Portland.* Both groups had floated down the Yukon River from the Klondike to the ocean port at St. Michaels, and the wealth they brought out seemed to confirm the rumors of a fantastic bonanza in the Far North. Overnight the nation went mad to be in contact with that remote country. Pierre Berton, the leading authority on the 1897 gold rush, writes that "there had been nothing like the Klondike before, there has been nothing like it since, and there can never be anything like it again."

Although there had been richer strikes (the extent of the gold field was grossly overestimated, and most of the bonanza claims would have been taken before the mob arrived), Berton points out that there had never been such a sudden and dramatic reaction: "The Klondike stampede did not start slowly and build up to a climax, as did so many earlier gold rushes. It started instantly with the arrival of the *Excelsior* and *Portland,* reached a fever pitch at once, and remained at fever pitch until the following spring, when, with the coming of the Spanish-American War, the fever died almost as swiftly as it arose. . . . It was the last and most frenzied of the great international gold rushes."[22]

Unlike the gold which only one in twenty of the stampeders

found, the reasons for the frenzy are readily discovered: we need look no further than the old familiar American Dream. Escape, romance, adventure, freedom, wealth, a second-chance—these were the motives behind the great stampede northward, just as they were the primary ingredients of the dream. The mood of unquiet desperation in America's response may also be understood, if not justified, by the times. The United States was still recovering from the worst depression of its history. The swelling of American cities after the Civil War; the spreading stain of poverty and slums; the suffocating railroad tariffs which imposed on the Western farmers all the traffic would bear; the squeezing out of the small independent businessman by the giant monopolies; the political corruption of "The Great Barbecue"; the moral hypocrisies and social affectations of the genteel mode—in short, revulsion against all the decadence of the Gilded Age galvanized the nation's yearning to recapture its lost youth.

Suddenly and unexpectedly the vast, mysterious Northland held forth one final splendid opportunity for a return to the paradisal wilderness—for Edenic rebirth, riches, and manhood. "I believed that I was about to see and take part in a most picturesque and impressive movement across the wilderness," Hamlin Garland reminisced; "I believed it to be the last march of the kind which could ever come to America, so rapidly were the wild places being settled up. . . . I wished to return to the wilderness also, to forget books and theories of art and social problems, and come again face to face with the great free spaces of woods, skies and streams."[23] Garland's confession is a fair representation of the mythic vision; small wonder, then, that before the turn of the century, disregarding the warnings of the cynics who branded them as a "horde of fools" suffering from acute "Klondicitis," a hundred thousand argonauts had struck out, boats against the current, under the mass illusion that the end of the great American rainbow was located somewhere near the junction of the Yukon and Klondike rivers.

Nor is it surprising that Jack London was among the first of the stampeders. Two years of schooling and drudgery had passed since he had returned from The Road, and he had little to show for his efforts except a few rejection slips. On July 25, Jack—along

with his brother-in-law, Captain J. H. Shepard, who had mort-
gaged his home for their stake—boarded the *Umatilla* for the
Klondike. "I had let career go hang," he wrote, "and was on
the adventure-path again in quest of fortune" (*John
Barleycorn*, 231).

Though London complained he brought nothing back from
the Klondike but scurvy and though it is apparently true that
he did not find anything but fool's gold, that year was in many
ways the richest investment of his life. His four-hundred-mile
trek from Dyea Beach over the rugged Chilkoot Pass, through
the dangerous White Horse Rapids, and downriver to the mouth
of the Stewart River, where he spent most of the winter, was
in itself the adventure of a lifetime—as was the two-thousand-
mile journey by raft down the great Yukon River the following
spring. But these personal experiences were a slim return in
comparison with the rich payload he mined during the long
Arctic night listening to the tales that passed between the
veteran "sourdoughs" and newly arrived "chechaquos." Many
of the stories that passed for fact were undoubtedly fictions
and glamorized truths, for—said Jack—"The Alaskan gold hunter
is proverbial, not so much for his unveracity, as for his inability
to tell the precise truth. In a country of exaggerations, he likewise is prone to hyperbolic descriptions of things actual. But
when it came to [the] Klondike, he could not stretch the truth
as fast as the truth itself stretched."[24] Pierre Berton indicates
that "there, if ever, was a classic case where the truth was far
stranger [than fiction]. The facts themselves are gaudy enough
for the wildest melodrama or the most compelling Odyssey.
It is foolish to try to improve upon them, and he who attempts
it does so at his peril."[25]

Yet Jack London was never one to be inhibited by the threat
of either peril or failure. During the long, dark winter he was
not merely collecting the raw materials that would be transmuted
into fictional character and narrative; he was absorbing the
very atmosphere of the Northland itself. As a result, and contrary to the usual critical assumptions about his work, his best
fiction would not rely primarily upon plot but, instead, would
derive its impact from what in "The Art of Fiction" Henry James
called "truth of detail," "the air of reality," "solidity of specifica-

tion"—"the merit on which all its other merits . . . helplessly and submissively depend." This special ambience would be largely responsible for the fact that, out of the more than one hundred books written about the Klondike gold rush, London's tales are virtually the only literary survivors three generations afterwards.

The physical consequences of the long winter of good comradeship and tale-swapping were less salutary. By the spring thaws the lack of exercise—coupled with a lack of fresh vegetables —was taking its toll. Jack's gums began to swell and bleed, and his teeth started to loosen and rattle in his head: the dread symptoms of "Arctic leprosy"—scurvy. As his condition worsened with aching joints and lameness, he decided that for himself the law of diminishing returns now governed his Klondike adventure. On June 8, 1898, while thousands of new stampeders were beginning to pour into the gold country after the long winter, Jack with two companions started home aboard a jerry-built houseboat on the Yukon River.

We need only look at a map of Alaska to appreciate the scope of this downriver journey. The Yukon is perhaps the world's most indecisive river. Its headwater lakes are located just north of Juneau, almost within a stone's throw of the Pacific Ocean. But, instead of taking the logical short route to the sea, it wanders northward for almost a thousand miles until it reaches the Arctic Circle, where, meeting the southwest-bound Porcupine, it changes course at an eighty-degree angle and heads toward the Bering Sea. Seven hundred miles later, after moving into Anvik southwest, it turns southeast to Holy Cross, hesitates and then wanders southwest for another hundred miles until it passes Russian Mission. Then, meandering the last hundred and fifty miles mostly northward, it oozes in countless channels across the great mud flats into Norton Sound. The Yukon is almost as long as, and in spots wider than, the Mississippi; and the land it traverses is still one of the wildest regions in North America, abundant with myriad forms of wildlife—where mosquitos swarm thickly enough, swear returning travelers, to darken the sky, suffocate pack animals, and drive men into hysteria.

London kept notebooks about his downriver journey, and he later published his story in *The Illustrated Buffalo Express* under the title "From Dawson to the Sea." A Northland variation of *Adventures of Huckleberry Finn*, the story is built upon the raft-as-home theme:

> Our boat was home-made, weak-kneed and leaky, but in thorough harmony with the wilderness we were traversing. . . . In the bow was the woodshed, while amidships, built of pine boughs and blankets was the bed chamber. Then came the rower's bench, and, jammed between this and the steersman, was our snug little kitchen. It was a veritable home, and we had little need of going ashore, save out of curiosity or to lay in a fresh supply of firewood.
>
> The three of us had sworn to make of this a pleasure trip, in which all labor was to be performed by gravitation, and all profit reaped by ourselves. And what a profit it was to us who had been accustomed to pack great loads on our backs or drag all day at the sleds for a paltry 25 or 30 miles. We now hunted, played cards, smoked, ate and slept, sure of our six miles an hour, of our 144 a day.[26]

Three weeks of this kind of drifting—punctuated by occasional stops at Indian villages and trading posts ashore—brought the raft and its crew to St. Michaels where London worked as a coalpasser aboard a steamer headed for San Francisco. A month later, in early August, 1898, he was home and was synthesizing the materials that would bring him the success he had resolved so desperately to achieve. By the time *The Call of the Wild* appeared in 1903, one hundred million dollars in gold dust and nuggets had been milked from the cold, muddy tributaries of the Yukon, and only a handful of mining engineers and inveterate sourdoughs were left in the ghostly wastelands and deserted boom towns to gather the residual deposits of the precious metal. Within less than a decade America's last frontier became a golden memory. No longer a material reality to excite men to frantic action, it was a rich lode for the writer who could tap its mythic bedrock and incite men to dream.

CHAPTER *2*

The Literary Frontiersman

To understand the opening years of the new century one must study Jack Londonism.
—Fred Lewis Pattee, *The Development of the American Short Story*

Avoid the unhappy ending, the harsh, the brutal, the tragic, the horrible—if you care to see in print the things you write. (In this connection don't do as I do, but do as I say.)
—Jack London, *The Editor*, March 1903

BECAUSE we have been conditioned by more than two generations of Realism, it is difficult to imagine the kind of fiction that dominated American magazines at the turn of the century. Perhaps the easiest way is to look at a few issues of the prestigious *Atlantic Monthly*. Volumes LXXXIV and LXXXV (1899 and 1900) disclose a genuine editorial concern for social and political relevance in the publication of such articles as Jacob A. Riis's series on the slums, Frank Norris's "Comida: An Experience in Famine" (an essay on the civilian war victims in Cuba), William James's *Talks to Teachers on Psychology*, and Prince Peter Kropotkin's *The Autobiography of a Revolutionist*. But the fiction in these volumes scarcely suggests such concern. For example, Mary Johnston's *To Have and To Hold*— a serialized historical romance which is reported to have doubled *Atlantic* circulation in 1900—is set in early seventeenth-century Virginia; and the action revolves about the love affair of Captain Ralph Percy and the lovely Jocelyn Leigh as they endure the tribulations of piracy, Indian savagery, and Lord Carnal's lecherous villainy. The following scene describes—in typical fashion—the hero's sentimental reverie as he lies awaiting death at the hands of his savage captors:

40

I was no babe to whimper at a sudden darkness, to cry out against a curtain that a Hand chose to drop between me and the life I had lived. Death frighted me not, but when I thought of one whom I should leave behind me I feared lest I should go mad. Had this thing come to me a year before, I could have slept the night through; now—now—

I lay, bound to the log, before the open door of the lodge, and, looking through it, saw the pines waving in the night wind and the gleam of the river beneath the stars, and saw her as plainly as though she had stood there under the trees, in a flood of noon sunshine. . . . One of my arms was free; I could take from within my doublet the little purple flower, and drop my face upon the hand that held it. The bloom was quite withered, and scalding tears would not give it life again.[1]

Another generation would pass before American readers were ready to appreciate the restraint of Hemingway.

If William Dean Howells's teacup therapy had not managed to rid the popular novel of such sugar-and-spice Romanticism, the short story—virtually ignored in Realist theory—was worse yet. In the August, 1899, issue of the *Atlantic,* for instance, Elizabeth Stuart Phelps's "Loveliness: A Story" begins typically: "Loveliness sat on an eider-down cushion embroidered with cherry-colored puppies on a pearl satin cover. . . . For Loveliness was a little dog. . . . the essence of tenderness; set, soul and body, to one only tune. To love and be beloved—that was his life." And, in the January, 1900, number Margaret L. Knapp's "Mother" ends just as typically, "Jack, dear heart, it was selfish in me to . . . leave you; but I had to do it,—I had to see my mother. Mother knows."

Such samples, culled from America's foremost literary magazine, help to explain why the period has been called "the Mauve Decade" and "the decade of arrested development." We should remember, in all fairness to the *Atlantic* editors, that this period was the same one in which Leo Tolstoi's *The Awakening* was bowdlerized by the editors of *Cosmopolitan,* Thomas Hardy's *Jude the Obscure* was expurgated in *Harper's* under the fetching title of *Hearts Insurgent,* and Theodore Dreiser's *Sister Carrie* was suppressed on grounds of impropriety by Doubleday, Page & Company. Into this literary hothouse Jack London entered as a bracing draft of Arctic air: "Except for the similar sensation

caused by the appearance of Mark Twain's mining-camp humor
in the midst of Victorian America, nothing more disturbing to
the forces of gentility had ever happened in our literature,"
Kenneth Lynn has written, "and it decisively changed the course
of American fiction."[2]

Jack scarcely saw himself in such a messianic role; he was
simply concerned with getting ahead in the world.

I Making It

Every magazine has its clique of writers, on whom it depends, and
whom it patronizes in preference to all other writers. . . . Well, a
newcomer must excel them in their own fields before he is accepted,
or else he must create a new field.   —Letters from Jack London (8)

In *John Barleycorn* London contended, "Some are born to
fortune, and some have fortune thrust upon them. But in my
case I was clubbed into fortune, and bitter necessity wielded
the club" (237-38). The financial situation at home was acute
when he returned from his Klondike trip in the summer of 1898.
Jack had many talents, but no skill or trade; and, though he
listed his name with five employment bureaus and advertised
in three newspapers, he could get no steady work, and was
reduced to odd jobs such as mowing lawns, trimming hedges,
and beating carpets. He scored high on the civil service examinations for postman, but there were no vacancies. In desperation
he turned once again to writing, not this time—or so he thought—
as a career, but merely to put bread on the table at home.
Figuring that the minimum pay for newspaper articles was ten
dollars, he sat down to organize an account of his downriver
exodus from the Klondike. "My honest intention in writing that
article," he insisted, "was to earn ten dollars. And that was the
limit of my intention. It would help to tide me along until I got
steady employment. Had a vacancy occurred in the post office
at that time, I should have jumped at it" (*John Barleycorn*, 238).

In September, he sent the following letter to the editor of
the San Francisco *Bulletin*:

Dear Sir:
  I have returned from a year's residence in the Clondyke [*sic*],
entering the country by way of Dyea and Chilcoot Pass. I left by

way of St. Michaels, thus making altogether a journey of 2,500 miles on the Yukon in a small boat. I have sailed and traveled quite extensively in other parts of the world and have learned to seize upon that which is interesting, to grasp the true romance of things, and to understand the people I may be thrown amongst.

I have just completed an article of 4,000 words, describing the trip from Dawson to St. Michaels in a rowboat. Kindly let me know if there would be any demand in your columns for it—of course, thoroughly understanding that the acceptance of the manuscript is to depend upon its literary and intrinsic value.

Yours very respectfully,
Jack London
(*Letters from Jack London,* 3)

In what would seem to have been one of the great blunders of publishing history, the editor returned the letter with a hasty reply scribbled on the bottom: "Interest in Alaska has subsided in an amazing degree. Then, again, so much has been written, that I do not think it would pay us to buy your story."[3]

Most important, however, in London's early letter is the disclosure of three essential factors which account in large measure for his success as a writer: (1) "to seize upon that which is interesting," (2) "to grasp the true romance of things," (3) "to understand the people I may be thrown amongst." Human interest, romantic imagination, sympathetic understanding: these are the major ingredients in his work and—combined with the forces of luck, talent, and plain "dig"—made him one of the most popular writers of his generation. Another element, which he did not mention and which, indeed, he seemed hardly aware of—a genius for myth—made his achievement ultimately something more lasting than popular success.

But during the bleak winter of 1898 such possibilities as success and fame seemed remote. Try as he would, Jack could not find steady employment; and, because he had no viable alternatives, he worked between odd jobs at a rented typewriter upon which he ground out articles, poems, jokes, stories—including a twenty-one-thousand-word serial for *Youth's Companion*; and he pawned his bike and winter suit to get stamps for mailing off his manuscripts, which were in turn mailed back with sickening regularity. Though frustrating, it was nonetheless a valuable time because it provided the intensive exercise he needed to acquire the professional touch. "I am unlearning and learning anew," he wrote to Mabel Applegarth on Thanksgiving weekend; "I shall subordinate thought to technique till the latter is mastered; then I shall do vice a versa." And he added a melancholy afterthought: "I do not know when I can be down—I may be digging sewers or shoveling coal next week" (*Letters from Jack London,* 4).

What he was actually doing next week was mulling over a letter from the *Overland Monthly,* the magazine founded and given nationwide prestige a generation earlier by Bret Harte. "We have read your MS.," the letter began, "and are so greatly pleased with it, that, though we have an enormous quantity of accepted and paid-for material on hand, we will at once publish it in the January number, if you can content yourself with five dollars."[4] Such acceptance might be a way to fame, but the fee would hardly make one's fortune. At five dollars for thirty-seven hundred words, he could in fact make more money digging sewers or shoveling coal. But, despite his disappointment, he accepted the *Overland* offer and continued to write. On December 25, 1898—"the loneliest Christmas I ever faced"—he vowed "an entire change of front" for the New Year: "I shall forsake my old dogmas, and henceforth, worship the true god. 'There is no God but Chance, and Luck shall be his prophet!' He who stops to think or beget a system is lost. As in other creeds, faith alone atones. Numerous hecatombs and many a fat firstling shall I sacrifice—you just watch my smoke (I beg pardon, I mean incense)" (*Letters from Jack London,* 9-11).

As his new God would have it, Jack passed his point of no return two months later when the Oakland postmaster telephoned to say there was a vacancy for mail carrier and London could have the job if he was ready to go to work. The starting pay would be sixty-five dollars a month—twice what he had made as a common laborer—with opportunities for regular increases, as well as security and retirement benefits. One month of delivering mail would pay more than he had made from five years of writing—unless he counted the check just received from the *Black Cat*: the incredible sum of forty dollars for a mediocre science-fiction tale titled "A Thousand Deaths," the kind of stuff he could now write with his eyes shut. Perhaps this sum was indicative of a real change in his luck; furthermore, his odds would be bettered by the deal offered him by *Overland* editor James Howard Bridge: if Jack would continue to produce stories as good as "To the Man on Trail" and "The White Silence," which would be published in the January and February, 1899, numbers, he would be given not only $7.50 a sketch but also prime space in the magazine. Although the prestige of "the Gold Coast *Atlantic*" had become slightly tarnished (Ambrose Bierce now referred to it as "the warmed-*Overland Monthly*"), it was still a big-name magazine and, despite its picayune fees, might serve as a springboard for an unknown young writer.

The prospects for literary success had never been more tantalizing; on the other hand, the pressure to accept the certain income and the excellent security of the government job was urgent. London tells in *John Barleycorn* how the dilemma was resolved for him:

> I couldn't decide what to do. And I'll never be able to forgive the postmaster of Oakland. I answered the call, and I talked to him like a man. I frankly told him the situation. . . . Now, if he would pass me by and select the next man on the eligible list, and give me a call at the next vacancy—
> But he shut me off with: "Then you don't want the position?"
> "But I do," I protested. "Don't you see, if you will pass me over this time—"
> "If you want it you will take it," he said coldly.
> Happily for me, the cursed brutality of the man made me angry. "Very well," I said. "I won't take it." (*John Barleycorn*, 239)

Had Chance decreed a vacancy ten days earlier, or a more civil postmaster, America might have gained another servant of the public mails, inadvertently relegating the name "Jack London" to the deadletter office. London should not merely have forgiven but should have thanked the postmaster of Oakland for angering him into pursuing his true calling.

Spring—the time of the open road—was approaching again; but this time the only road left open to Jack led him to success in the world of belles-lettres. That road is charted in two thumb-worn nickel composition books now secured under double lock in the Utah State University Library and simply labeled:

NO. 1   NO. 2
MAGAZINE SALES   MAGAZINE SALES
FROM 1898 TO MAY 1900   FROM MAY 1900 TO FEB. 1903

These two unpretentious notebooks not only confirm the legend
of London's fabulous rise to success; they also tell, as King
Hendricks has pointed out, "a graphic story of feverish work,
disappointments and frustrations and of the tenacious determination to succeed."[5]

Notebook No. 1, more noteworthy for its number of failures
than its successes, reveals that London quite probably holds the
record as America's most rejected author. Of the one hundred
and three items listed, only fifty-seven were accepted for publication; and of these fifty-seven, only fifteen were accepted the
first time they were submitted. Of the remainder, more than
thirty items were permanently "retired" after multiple rejections; four were lost; and another four were rewritten and carried
over to the second notebook. The one hundred and three items
in the first book garnered more than four hundred rejections.

What is most impressive about these entries, in addition to
the author's amazing persistence, is their variety: short stories,
sonnets, triolets, humorous sketches, jokes, essays on subjects
ranging from grammar to economics—anything, in short, that
might sell for fifty cents upwards. This joke, for instance, was
sent to seven different periodicals before retirement:

Mike.—An' what's the matter wid yer arm?
Pat.—Sure, an' the Docther sez it's compound fracture, but it's meself
     belaves the bones is broken.

Surprisingly, some of this stuff did sell. The following triolet was
accepted by *Town Topics* in May, 1900, after having been rejected eleven times (including a rejection by *Town Topics* a
year earlier):

When he came in,
    Why, I was out.
To borrow some tin
Was why he came in,

> And I had to grin,
> For he was without;
> So I was in,
> And he was out.

London later used the poem, slightly modified, as an example of Martin Eden's early hack work: "It's not art," Martin admits to Ruth Morse, "but it's a dollar." The dollar that Jack got for the poem barely enabled him to break even on the postage and envelopes invested in circulating the poem for publication. Marking the end of the first third of the book, this triolet is pivotal. Up to this point the retirement-acceptance ratio is two to one in favor of retirement; in the rest of the book, the ratio is almost exactly reversed—acceptances outnumber retirements better than two to one. The trend is confirmed in Notebook No. 2, thereby indicating that London had by May, 1900, found out his strengths and weaknesses. Gone are the crippled verses and lame jokes. More than half of the seventy-two entries are short stories; the rest are sketches and essays. Of these seventy-two, only two were retired, and one of these was later resurrected for publication in a book of London's essays.

One of the most significant entries in either notebook is the fifty-third item in Notebook No. 1: "An Odyssey of the North," mailed to the *Atlantic Monthly* on June 10, 1899. Two days later Jack complained to his literary pen-pal Cloudesley Johns, "I am groping, groping, groping for my own particular style, for the style which should be mine but which I have not yet found" (*Letters from Jack London*, 42). Six weeks later the *Atlantic* returned "An Odyssey of the North" with the note that, if he would shorten the manuscript by three thousand words, the story would be accepted. On August 1, he sent back the revised story; and on October 30 he received a check for one hundred and twenty dollars and also a complimentary one-year subscription.

Acceptance by America's premier literary monthly signified a major breakthrough. The *Overland Monthly* had provided literary respectability, and the *Black Cat* had given financial reassurance. The *Atlantic* gave Jack these things and something even more valuable: self-confidence. Henceforth there would be no further groping for his own particular style. What was good

enough for the *Atlantic* was surely good enough for the rest.
By the winter of 1899, when he signed the contract with Houghton Mifflin for his first book—a collection of the eight Klondike
stories which had appeared in the *Overland*, along with "An
Odyssey of the North"—London had abandoned the amateurish
frenzy of his early writings and had settled into the steady professional pace he maintained for the rest of his life. "Am now
doing a thousand words per day, six days a week," he wrote to
Johns. "Last week I finished 1100 words ahead of the required
amount. To-day (Tuesday), I am 172 ahead of my stint. I have
made it a rule to make up next day what I fall behind; but
when I run ahead, to not permit it to count on the following
day. I am sure a man can turn out more, and much better in
the long run working this way, than if he works by fits and
starts" (*Letters from Jack London*, 60). And by the time
Houghton Mifflin released *The Son of the Wolf* in the spring
of 1900, he had set not only the routine but also the style which
would remain essentially unchanged throughout the rest of his
career. "Let me tell you how I write," he explained in a letter
to Elwyn Hoffman, another early fan. "In the first place I never
begin a thing, but what I finish *before* I begin anything else.
Further; I type as fast as I write, so that each day sees the work
all upon the final MS. which goes for editorial submission. And
on the day I finish the MS. I fold it up and send it off without
once going back to see what all the previous pages were like.
So, in fact, when a page is done, that is the last I see of it till
it comes out in print."[6] This remarkable facility explains in part
why it was that London had so little regard for much of his
work and why there is so little change in his style. The changes
had already taken place, for the most part, in the period of
feverish apprenticeship before his first book appeared on the
market.

Later, answering the critics who had raised their eyebrows
over the incredible success of his hero in *Martin Eden*, London
asserted, "In three years, from a sailor with a common school
education, I made a successful writer of him. The critics say this
is impossible. Yet I was Martin Eden. At the end of three working years, two of which were spent in high school and the
university and one spent at writing, and all three in studying

immensely and intensely, I was publishing stories in magazines such as the *Atlantic Monthly*, was correcting proofs of my first book . . . , was selling sociological articles to *Cosmopolitan* and *McClure's,* had declined an associate editorship proffered me by telegraph from New York City, and was getting ready to marry" (*John Barleycorn,* p. 242). London's success was an extraordinary literary phenomenon, and it occurred because his hard-earned mastery of narrative technique and his instinctive genius for myth meshed precisely with a change in cultural tastes and with the sudden national awareness that the frontier and all its dreams of glory were gone.

II   *The Northland Saga*

His gallery of supermen and superwomen has about it the myth atmosphere of the older world. . . . It is a new Northern mythology, and the stories . . . have the quality of sagas. Contrary to his own belief, [London] was not a realist at all. His tales were not written on the spot, but after they had mellowed for years in his imagination. Everywhere exaggerations, poetizations, utter marvels described as commonplaces, superlatives in every sentence. It is not the actual North; it is an epic dream of the North, colored by an imagination adolescent in its love of the marvelous, of fighting and action, and of headlong movement.
         —F. L. Pattee, *The Development of the American Short Story*

Specific titles of London's works may be blurred among our other dim memories of youth, but few persons who have ever encountered his tales can totally forget the lonely traveler who dies unmourned in the awesome cold of the Arctic winter because he has accidentally wet his feet and failed to build a fire; the lost miner who wanders across the Arctic waste land in a nightmarish odyssey of starvation and exposure, sustained solely by an incredible will to live; or either of the magnificent dogs: Buck, captivated by the call of the Northland Wild, and White Fang, tamed by the loving-kindness of a gentler master. There is something timeless about these stories. At the turn of the century, when they first appeared, there was also something very timely about them.

A reading public that had dieted on propriety and pap for more

than a generation and whose appetite for strenuous action had
been whetted by the colorful melodramas of Kipling and by
the melodramatics of Theodore Roosevelt was hungry for the
meaty fare of Jack London's Northland. The opening sentence
of "An Odyssey of the North" is the harbinger of a new kind of
American fiction: "The sleds were singing their eternal lament
to the creaking of the harnesses and the tinkling bells of the
leaders; but the men and dogs were tired and made no sound."[7]
Others had already used the Klondike materials for profit, but
their writings lacked the vividness and poetic cadence of London's style, a style which fused the vigorous and the picturesque.
Furthermore, his was a fresh breed of fictional heroes—not the
maudlin gentlemen who scalded flowers with their tears or who
emasculated themselves on the altars of sentimental caprice—
but "a lean and wiry type, with trail-hardened muscles, and
sun-browned faces, and untroubled souls which gazed frankly
forth, clear-eyed and steady" (Son of the Wolf, 192-93). Kipling
had introduced a kindred type the decade before, and London
was quick to acknowledge his debt to the master of the
"plain tale."[8]

But the Klondike argonauts were not merely copies of those
leathery cockneys and Irishmen in the Queen's Army whose
individualism was subverted to the uses of British Imperialism
and whose sporting ethic was at times gratuitously cruel. London's Northland heroes were, by contrast, a ruggedly independent yet a remarkably compassionate breed who paid allegiance
only to the inexorable laws of nature and to the authority of
conscience, but who also possessed a capacity for selflessness
and comradeship very much like the agape of primitive Chris-
tianity. Theirs was a situational ethic, predicated on integrity,
charity, and pragmatism. They had invaded a hostile land where
the ruling law was "survival of the fittest" and where the key
to survival was adaptability, but this did not simply mean
physical fitness or brute strength: "The man who turns his back
upon the comforts of an elder civilization, to face the savage
youth, the primordial simplicity of the North, may estimate
success at an inverse ratio to the quantity and quality of his
hopelessly fixed habits," explains the narrator in his prologue
to the story "In a Far Country":

The exchange of such things as a dainty menu for rough fare, of the stiff leather shoe for the soft, shapeless moccasin, of the feather bed for a couch in the snow, is after all a very easy matter. But his pinch will come in learning properly to shape his mind's attitude toward all things, and especially toward his fellow man. For the courtesies of ordinary life, he must substitute unselfishness, forbearance, and tolerance. Thus, and thus only, can he gain that pearl of great price, —true comradeship. He must not say "Thank you"; he must mean it without opening his mouth, and prove it by responding in kind. In short, he must substitute the deed for the word, the spirit for the letter.   (*Son of the Wolf,* 70)

This code of the Northland, with the mystique of comrade-ship at its heart, is dramatized in "To the Man on Trail," the first of Jack's Klondike stories which had so excited the editors of the *Overland Monthly.* A Yuletide story, it is trimmed with the rich assortment of symbols, pagan as well as Christian, appropriate to the occasion. The setting is Christmas Eve in the cabin of the Malemute Kid, who dominates *The Son of the Wolf* collection as high priest of the code. Gathered together are representatives from a dozen different lands who are swapping yarns, reminiscing about home, and sharing the heady Christmas punch concocted by Kid. At midnight the conviviali-ties are suddenly interrupted by the jingling of bells, "the familiar music of the dogwhip, the whining howl of the Male-mutes, and the crunch of a sled"; then comes "the expected knock, sharp and confident" and the entrance of "the stranger": ". . . a striking personage, and a most picturesque one, in his Arctic dress of wool and fur. Standing six foot two or three, with proportionate breadth of shoulders and depth of chest, . . . his long lashes and eyebrows white with ice, . . . he seemed, of a verity, the Frost King, just stepped in out of the night. . . . An awkward silence had fallen, but his hearty 'What cheer, my lads?' put them quickly at ease, and the next instant Malemute Kid and he had gripped hands. Though they had never met, each had heard of the other, and the recognition was mutual" (*Son of the Wolf,* 105-7).

The apparition suggests Saint Nicholas himself—but in a peculiar Klondike guise. He has been on the frozen trail for twelve hours running, and he is burdened, not with the traditional sack of gifts, but, instead, with "two large Colt's revolvers and a hunting-knife ... the inevitable dogwhip, a smokeless rifle of the largest bore and latest pattern" (106). Jack Weston-dale, the stranger, explains that he is pursuing a gang of dog thieves. While the guest is eating the Christmas snack hospitably prepared for him, Kid studies his face and finds him worthy:

Nor was he long in deciding that it was fair, honest, and open, and that he liked it. Still youthful, the lines had been firmly traced by toil and hardship. Though genial in conversation, and mild when at rest, the blue eyes gave promise of the hard steel-glitter which comes when called into action, especially against odds. The heavy jaw and square-cut chin demonstrated rugged pertinacity and indom-itability. Nor, though the attributes of the lion were there, was there wanting the certain softness, the hint of womanliness, which bespoke the emotional nature. (108)

Westondale apparently embodies all the vital traits of the code hero; and, while he is taking a quick nap before again taking to the trail, the impression is confirmed by Kid: "Been in going on three years, with nothing but the name of working like a horse, and any amount of bad luck to his credit.... The trouble with him is clean grit and stubbornness" (111). A short three hours later Kid rouses the young giant and—Magus-like—sends him on his way with fresh provisions and wise counsel. Fifteen minutes later the festivities are stopped a second time—by a nearly exhausted stranger who wears the red coat, not of St. Nick, but of the Royal Canadian Mounted Police. He de-mands fresh dogs and information about Westondale, who is running—he discloses—not for, but *from,* the law after having robbed a Dawson gambling casino of forty thousand dollars!

Though the revelers have kept silent according to Kid's example, they furiously demand an explanation after the Mountie has gone: why has Kid given sanctuary and aid to a man who has doubly violated the code by robbery and by deception?

"It's a cold night, boys,—a bitter cold night," was the irrelevant commencement of his defense. "You've all traveled trail, and know what that stands for. Don't jump a dog when he's down. You've only heard one side. A whiter man than Jack Westondale never ate from the same pot nor stretched blanket with you or me. Last fall he gave his whole clean-up, forty thousand, to Joe Castrell, to buy in on Dominion. To-day he'd be a millionaire. But while he stayed behind at Circle City, taking care of his partner with the scurvy, what does Castrell do? Goes into McFarland's, jumps the limit, and drops the whole sack. Found him dead in the snow the next day. And poor Jack laying his plans to go out this winter to his wife and the boy he's never seen. You'll notice he took exactly what his partner lost,—forty thousand. Well, he's gone out; and what are you going to do about it?"

The Kid glanced around the circle of his judges, noted the softening of their faces, then raised his mug aloft. "So a health to the man on trail this night; may his grub hold out; may his dogs keep their legs; may his matches never miss fire. God prosper him; good luck go with him; and"—

"Confusion to the Mounted Police!" cried Bettles, to the crash of the empty cups. (117–18)

Without belaboring his symbolism, London has provided a fitting epiphany to the conclusion of his Christmas carol; moreover, the situational ethic which informs the story was sure to appeal to a reading public less than one generation removed from frontier justice.

The mystique of comradeship is obversely dramatized in the fourth story in *The Son of the Wolf* collection, "In a Far Country," which had first appeared in the June, 1899, issue of the *Overland Monthly*. In this tale about "two Incapables" named Carter Weatherbee and Percy Cuthfert, who elect to spend the long Arctic winter snugly marooned in a deserted cabin rather than suffer the hardships of breaking trail with their comrades for the thousand remaining miles to Dawson, London reiterates the idea that survival is not primarily a matter of physical fitness.

Both Incapables are healthy, husky men, whereas Merritt Sloper, the wiry little argonaut who functions as moral norm in this and in several other Klondike episodes, weighs less than a hundred pounds and is still yellow and weak from the fever he had picked up in South America: "The fresh young muscles of either Weatherbee or Cuthfert were equal to ten times the endeavor of his; yet he could walk them into the earth in a day's journey.... He was the incarnation of the unrest of his race, and the old Teutonic stubbornness, dashed with the quick grasp and action of the Yankee, held the flesh in the bondage of the spirit" (77-78). Sloper predicts the Incapables' fate as he and the remaining members of the party pull out from the cabin: "[Ever] hear of the Kilkenny cats?" he asks Jacques Baptiste, the party's half-breed guide. "Well, my friend and good comrade, the Kilkenny cats fought till neither hide, nor hair, nor yowl, was left. . . . Now, these two men don't like work. They won't work. We know that. They'll be all alone in that cabin all winter,—a mighty long, dark winter" (80).

At first, Sloper's prophecy appears to be wrong, for the Incapables seem determined to prove their compatibility; in addition, they are plentifully stocked with food and fuel. But, representatives of a degenerate society, they are fatally undersupplied in the moral staples needed for subsistence in the Northland. Weatherbee, formerly a clerk, is an unimaginative, materialistic fool who has joined the gold rush to make his fortune; Cuthfert, opposite as well as apposite, is the overripe cultural dilettante afflicted with "an abnormal development of sentimentality [which he mistakes] for the true spirit of romance and adventure" (72). Moreover, the two men lack that "protean faculty of adaptability"—the capacity to slough off the callus of "self" along with the specious comforts of civilization—which is the most vital insurance against the dangers of the wilderness.

After an overeager show of industrious cooperation, they abandon the austere discipline of the code. Their spiritual degeneration, as they succumb to each of the Seven Deadly Sins, is initially dramatized in their social relationship. First, pride is manifest in a foolish arrogance which precludes the mutual trust requisite to survival in the wilderness: "Save existence, they had nothing in common,—came in touch on no single point. Weatherbee was a clerk who had known naught but clerking all his life; Cuthfert was a master of arts, a dabbler in oils, and had written not a little. The one was a lower-class man who considered himself a gentleman, and the other was a gentleman who knew himself to be such. From this it may be remarked that a man can be a gentleman without possessing the first instinct of true comradeship. . . . He deemed the clerk a filthy, uncultured brute whose place was in the muck with the swine, and told him so;

and he was reciprocally informed that he was a milk-and-water sissy and a cad" (82-83).

Next appears lust, as they consume with sensual promiscuity their supply of sugar, mixing it with hot water and then dissipating "the rich, white syrup" over their flapjacks and breadcrusts. This is followed by sloth, as they sink into a lethargy which makes them "rebel at the performance of the smallest chore," including washing and personal cleanliness—"and for that matter, common decency" (84-85). Accelerated by gluttony, their moral deterioration now begins to externalize itself in their physical appearance:

As the sugarpile and other little luxuries dwindled, they began to be afraid they were not getting their proper shares, and in order that they might not be robbed, they fell to gorging themselves. The luxuries suffered in this gluttonous contest, as did also the men. In the absence of fresh vegetables and exercise, their blood became impoverished, and a loathsome, purplish rash crept over their bodies. . . . Next, their muscles and joints began to swell, the flesh turning black, while their mouths, gums, and lips took on the color of rich cream. Instead of being drawn together by their misery, each gloated over the other's symptoms as the scurvy took its course. (85)

Covetousness and envy appear when they divide their sugar supply and hide their shares from each other, obsessed with the fear of losing the precious stuff.

The last of the cardinal sins, anger, is delayed awhile by another trouble: "the Fear of the North. . . . the joint child of the Great Cold and the Great Silence" (86), which preoccupies each man according to his nature. For the dilettantish Cuthfert, the Fear manifests itself quietly and inwardly: "He dwelt upon the unseen and unknown till the burden of eternity appeared to be crushing him. Everything in the Northland had that crushing effect,—the absence of life and motion; the darkness; the infinite peace of the brooding land; the ghastly silence, which made the echo of each heart-beat a sacrilege; the solemn forest which seemed to guard an awful, inexpressible something, which neither word nor thought could compass" (88). The coarser sensibilities of the clerk are more sensationally aroused in necrophilic nightmares: "Weatherbee fell prey to the grosser superstitions, and did his best to resurrect the spirits which slept in the forgotten graves. It was a fascinating thing, and in his dreams they came to him from out of the cold, and snuggled into his blankets. . . . He shrank from their clammy contact as they drew closer and twined their frozen limbs about him, and when they whispered in his ear of things to come, the cabin rang with his frightened shrieks" (86-87).

The symbolism grows richer as the drama moves toward its ghastly climax. Though London had not yet read the works of Sigmund Freud, his metaphors reveal an instinctive grasp of dream symbolism, particularly of the unconscious associations of sexual impotency and death. Cuthfert is obsessed with the absolute stillness of the phallic, arrow-shaped weathervane atop the cabin: "Standing beneath the wind-vane, his eyes fixed on the polar skies, he could not bring himself to realize that the Southland really existed, that at that very moment it was a-roar with life and action. There was no Southland, no men being born of women, no giving and taking in marriage. . . . He lived with Death among the dead, emasculated by the sense of his own insignificance . . ." (88-89). The metaphors of potency-life versus emasculation-death coalesce in the story's vivid climax, as anger completes the allegoric procession of the deadly sins. Thinking that his companion has pilfered his last tiny cache of the symbol-laden sugar, Weatherbee attacks Cuthfert in the cold fury of insanity and severs his spine with an axe, thereby fulfilling the premonition of symbolic emasculation; and then falls heavily upon him as the bullet from his victim's Smith & Weston explodes in his face.

The closing tableau—a grotesque inversion of the primal scene—dramatically reveals London's pre-Freudian intuitions: "The sharp bite of the axe had caused Cuthfert to drop the pistol, and as his lungs panted for release, he fumbled aimlessly for it among the blankets. Then he remembered. He slid a hand up the clerk's belt to the sheath-knife; and they drew very close to each other in that last clinch" (98). Passages like this one apparently substantiate Maxwell Geismar's observation that London seemed to be more at home in the "world of dream and fantasy and desolate, abnormal emotion . . . than the world of people and society" and that "his best work was often a transcript of solitary nightmares."[9] But such an assessment, notwithstanding the brilliance of Geismar's Freudian interpretation of London's life and work, is too limited. Though a considerable amount of his fiction does fit into this category, London's best is something more than "a transcript of solitary nightmares": it is the artistic modulation of universal dreams—*i.e.*, of myths and archetypes.

III *The Primordial Vision*

"Thus, on the Trail of the Gods we pass from life to life, and the gods know only and understand. Dreams and the shadows of dreams be memories, nothing more."   —Jack London, *Children of the Frost*

"A great work of art is like a dream," explains Carl Jung in *Modern Man in Search of a Soul*; "for all its apparent obviousness it does not explain itself and is never unequivocal. A dream never says: 'You ought,' or 'This is the truth.' It presents an image in much the same way as nature allows a plant to grow, and we must draw our own conclusions."[10] In his essay "Psychology and Literature" Jung draws a sharp line between the fundamental approaches of the artist: the "psychological mode" and the "visionary mode." The former, rational and objective, always takes its materials from the vast realm of conscious human experience: "Even the basic experiences themselves, though non-rational . . . are that which has been known from the beginnings of time—passion and its fated outcome, man's subjection to the turns of destiny, eternal nature with its beauty and its horror" (156).

The visionary mode "reverses all the conditions of the former. The experience that furnishes the material for artistic expression is no longer familiar. It is a strange something that derives its existence from the hinterland of man's mind—that suggests the abyss of time separating us from pre-human ages, or evokes a super-human world of contrasting light and darkness. It is a primordial experience which surpasses man's understanding. . . . We are reminded of nothing of everyday, human life, but rather of dreams, night-time fears and the dark recesses of the mind that we sometimes sense with misgiving" (156-58). In other

words, the visionary mode derives its materials from what Jung
calls the "collective unconscious": the deep psychological reser-
voir of "racial memories" that transcend both personal consciousness and the individual unconsciousness—or, as he explains,
"a certain psychic disposition shaped by the forces of heredity
[from which] consciousness has developed."

Because the language of normal discourse is inadequate to
express such visions, the artist must resort to the metaphorical
language of symbol and myth: "The primordial experience is
the source of his creativeness; it cannot be fathomed, and therefore requires mythological imagery to give it form. In itself it
offers no words or images, for it is a vision seen 'as in a glass,
darkly.' It is merely a deep presentiment that strives to find
expression" (164). The work of the visionary artist will therefore be informed by what Jung elsewhere calls "archetypes":
symbols of such transcendent and universal force that they
would seem to be instinctual predispositions toward certain
forms of psychic response rather than simple conditioned or
learned responses.[11] "The secret of artistic creation and of the
effectiveness of art," concludes Jung, "is to be found in a return
to the state of *participation mystique*—to that level of experience
at which it is man who lives, and not the individual, and at which
the weal or woe of the single human being does not count, but
only human existence" (172). Philip Young has put the case
somewhat more simply in defining myths as "stories which have
something about them that we clumsily call 'magic.' "

They have a special quality, an aura of portent. They deal, normally,
with some critical phase of life, some crisis. The figures who undergo
the adventures of the tale take on a symbolic air because we begin
to recognize in them some element of ourselves, and in their experience some aspect of our own. In an imaginative way we participate
in myths, and the more we are able to do this, the more meaning
they have for us. Of course we know that myths are false, as matters
of fact. But they can be so profound as matters of metaphor that
they make the facts seem superficial, and even accidental.[12]

One of the many ironies of Jack London's career is that he
thought of himself as a thoroughly professional craftsman working quite consciously in what Jung would have termed the

"psychological mode"; but, while most of his works can be superficially thus categorized, those with the most enduring force derive their potency from his instinctive mythopoeic vision. Readily apparent in the great fiction like "To Build a Fire" and *The Call of the Wild*, evidence of the visionary and mythic may be traced throughout the Northland Saga. In an obscure tale like "In the Forests of the North," for example, the hero is described as undergoing a "weary journey beyond the last scrub timber and straggling copses, into the heart of the Barrens. . . . the bad lands of the Arctic, the deserts of the Circle, the bleak and bitter home of the musk-ox and lean plains wolf. . . . treeless and cheerless" and beyond this across "the white blank spaces on the map" into a weird hyperborean region where he finds "undreamed-of rich spruce forests and unrecorded Eskimo tribes."[13] Long journeys far beyond the last outposts of civilization that penetrate into the great blank places—mysterious quests deep into the *urwelt,* the elder world of racial memories beyond space and time—form the recurrent pattern of the Northland Saga; and even the unimaginative reader may sense that such journeys reach beyond the material world.

"In the saga," Mircea Eliade explains, "the hero is placed in a world governed by the gods and fate."[14] In this same world London has placed his sourdoughs, Indians, and *chechaquos*; and the ruling gods are not flatly indifferent ones like the typical deities of Naturalistic literature; they are actively hostile and sometimes vengeful. In dramatizing these forces London's vision is essentially primordial rather than logical or "psychological," and the mode of his fiction is often symbolic rather than discursive. At his best, he reaches the level of other great American symbolists like Poe, Hawthorne, and Melville; and his primitive sensitivity to archetypes gives him a special affinity to Melville.

IV *The White Silence*

Is it that by its indefiniteness it shadows forth the heartless voids and immensities of the universe, and thus stabs us from behind with the thought of annihilation, when beholding the white depths of the milky way? Or is it, that as in essence whiteness is not so much a color as the visible absence of color, and at the same time the concrete of all colors; is it for these reasons that there is such a dumb blankness, full of meaning, in a wide landscape of snows—a colorless, all-color of atheism from which we shrink?

—Herman Melville, *Moby-Dick*

"It was very natural. Death came by many ways, yet was it all one after all,—a manifestation of the all-powerful and inscrutable."

—Jack London, *The God of His Fathers*

In his brilliant study of the symbolic mode in primitivism, James Baird identifies the "authentic primitivist" as an extreme individualist, as "the egoist-romanticist, as Santayana has described him . . . who 'disowns all authority save that mysteriously exercised over him by his deep faith in himself,' the man who would be 'heir to all civilization, and, nevertheless . . . take life arrogantly and egotistically, as if it were an absolute personal experiment,'" a man who will "entertain the idea of God in every form" and who will demonstrate "the custom of making symbols for the meaning of his own existence before a God whose nature he sees as inscrutable."[15] Sensing that the traditional symbols of his spiritually impoverished civilization have lost their potency, the primitivist will attempt to replace these with symbols derived from his own personal experience and from "the richest and least exhaustible alien cultures," particularly those of Polynesia and the Orient: "The symbolist's awareness of cultural failure becomes *atavism*, reversion, thoroughly dependent upon feeling, to the past in search for a prototypic culture. This atavism . . . permits the use of archetypal concepts in the making of new and 'personal' religious symbols" (17-18).

This definition applies to Jack London as well as to Herman Melville.[16] For all London's insistence on Realism, he was a blatant Romantic and an arrogant, inner-directed egoist with a profound faith in his own resources, who lived life as if it were "an absolute personal experiment." Born into an age when the larger religious structures of Western Civilization were tottering, and reared in a home without any formal religious orientation, London gravitated logically toward the secular doctrines of Karl Marx and Herbert Spencer; and he described himself as a revolutionary Socialist and as a materialistic monist. In theory, he generally managed to remain true to these faiths;

in practice, however, he demonstrated time and again that he was an individualist and a dualist. And an instinctive mysticism, not a logical positivism, dominates his Northland fiction. An example is the following passage from "The White Silence," the first story in *The Son of the Wolf*:

> The afternoon wore on, and with the awe, born of the White Silence, the voiceless travelers bent to their work. Nature has many tricks wherewith she convinces man of his finity,—the ceaseless flow of the tides, the fury of the storm, the shock of the earthquake, the long roll of heaven's artillery,—but the most tremendous, the most stupefying of all, is the passive phase of the White Silence. All movement ceases, the sky clears, the heavens are as brass; the slightest whisper seems sacrilege, and man becomes timid, affrighted at the sound of his own voice. Sole speck of life journeying across the ghostly wastes of a dead world, he trembles at his audacity, realizes that his is a maggot's life, nothing more. Strange thoughts arise unsummoned, and the mystery of all things strives for utterance. And the fear of death, of God, of the universe, comes over him,—the hope of the Resurrection and the Life, the yearning for immortality, the vain striving of the imprisoned essence,—it is then, if ever, man walks alone with God. (6–7)

London's Northland Deity, like the "inscrutable tides of God" in Melville's *Moby-Dick*, is the polar opposite of the philanthropic God-in-Nature celebrated by such sentimental "exoticists" as Jean Jacques Rousseau and François René de Chateaubriand.

Furthermore, in conveying the awesome ruthlessness of this deity, London drew his metaphors from the same mythic stockpile that Melville had used a half-century before him. Melville had fashioned his own unique metaphor, or "autotype," by combining two archetypes: the *fish*, an ancient life-symbol of divine creative force and wisdom, and *whiteness*, the emblematic all-color of universal mystery and the metonymy for an impersonal, incomprehensible deity of infinite paradoxes and incommunicable truth. "As one approaches the greatest of all Melville's symbols in the White Whale," says Baird, "he sees the greatest of Melville's answers (and the answers of all true primitivists) written in the stars: God is in himself multifarious and contradictory" (*Ishmael*, 234). For London, as for Melville, whiteness becomes "the most meaning symbol of spiritual

things, ... the intensifying agent in things the most appalling
to mankind" (*Moby-Dick*, Chapter 42).

But where Melville had combined whiteness with the fish, an
archetype of creation and the life-force, London fused it with
images of space, silence, and cold—and he thereby created an
autotype more subtly terrifying than the warm-blooded whale.
"*Le silence éternel de ces espaces infinis m'effraie*," mused Pascal.
And London's contemporary W. H. Hudson sensed the peculiar
affective quality of snow when he described it as

perhaps the most impressive [and] certainly one of the most widely
known [phenomena] on the earth, ... most intimately associated in
the mind with the yearly suspension of nature's beneficent activity,
and all that this means to the human family—the failure of food
and consequent want, and the suffering and danger from intense
cold. [Nature's] sweet friendly warmth and softness have died out
of it; there is no longer any recognition, any bond; and if we were
to fall down and perish by the wayside, there would be no compassion: it is sitting apart and solitary, cold and repelling, its breath
suspended, in a trance ... and although it sees us it is as though
it saw us not, even as we see pebbles and withered leaves on the
ground ... when some deadly purpose is in our heart.[17]

This suggestion of "deadly purpose," of an unnerving sentience,
is what most appalls in the White Silence. Cuthfert in "In a Far
Country" is reduced to craven depression by "the ghastly silence
[of] the solemn forest which seemed to guard an awful inexpressible something, which neither word nor thought could compass" (*Son of the Wolf*, 88). Still more explicit is the opening
section of *White Fang*: "A vast silence reigned over the land.
The land itself was a desolation, lifeless, without movement,
so lone and cold that the spirit of it was not even that of
sadness. There was a hint of laughter, but of a laughter more
terrible than any sadness—a laughter that was mirthless as the
smile of the Sphinx, a laughter cold as the frost and partaking
of the grimness of infallibility. It was the masterful and incommunicable wisdom of eternity laughing at the futility of life and
the effort of life." Thus conceived, London's White Silence is
not merely a convenient setting for adventurous plots; it emerges
as a dramatic antagonist charged with the special potency of
universal dream symbolism—that is, of myth.

This potency is displayed nowhere to better advantage than in "To Build a Fire," a masterpiece of short fiction which has become one of the most widely anthologized works ever produced by an American author. The central motif is simple enough, as London himself suggested: "Man after man in the Klondike has died alone after getting his feet wet, through failure to build a fire" (*Letters from Jack London*, 274). Plot and characterization are equally uncomplicated: a nameless *chechaquo* (newcomer to the Northland), accompanied by a large husky, is taking a day's hike across the frozen wilderness to join his partners at their mining claim. Although he has been warned by the old-timers against traveling alone in the White Silence, he, a strong, practical man, is confident of his ability to cope with the forces of nature. Yet we sense from the outset that he is doomed, as the narrator begins to weave his dark spell: "Day had broken cold and gray, exceedingly cold and gray, when the man turned aside from the main Yukon trail and climbed the high earth-bank, where a dim and little-traveled trail led eastward through the fat spruce timberland."

The key to the story's impact is not plot, but—as in much of London's best work—mood and atmosphere, which is conveyed through repetitive imagery of cold and gloom and whiteness: "There was no sun nor hint of sun, though there was not a cloud in the sky. It was a clear day, and yet there seemed an intangible pall over the face of things, a subtle gloom that made the day dark, and that was due to the absence of sun.... The man flung a look back along the way he had come. The Yukon lay a mile wide and hidden under three feet of ice. On top of this ice were as many feet of snow. It was all pure white.... North and south, as far as his eye could see, it was unbroken white, save for a dark hair-line [trail]."[18]

London's story manifests in its stark eloquence many of those same elements that Aristotle indicated in his *Poetics* as requisite to tragedy. It is a representation of an action that is serious, whole, complete, and of a certain magnitude. The action is rigorously unified, taking place between daybreak and nightfall. The protagonist, neither an especially good man nor an especially bad man, falls into misfortune because of a tragic flaw, notably hubris: an overweening confidence in the efficacy

of his own rational faculties and a corresponding blindness to
the dark, nonrational powers of nature, chance, and fate—

But all of this—the mysterious, far-reaching hair-line trail, the absence
of sun from the sky, the tremendous cold, and the strangeness and
weirdness of it all—made no impression on the man. . . . He was
quick and alert in the things of life, but only in the things, and not
in the significances. Fifty degrees below zero meant eighty-odd
degrees of frost. Such fact impressed him as being cold and un-
comfortable, and that was all. It did not lead him to meditate upon
his frailty as a creature of temperature, and upon man's frailty in
general, able only to live within certain narrow limits of heat and
cold; and from there on it did not lead him to the conjectural field
of immortality and man's place in the universe. (64–65)

Here, as throughout the story, the narrator functions as the
chorus, who mediates between the action and the reader and who
provides moral commentary upon the action. The setting, a mask
of the scornful gods, functions as antagonist. Aside from these,
the only other character is the dog, who acts as foil or "reflec-
tor" by displaying the humility and natural wisdom which the
man fatally lacks:

Its instinct told it a truer tale than was told to the man by the
man's judgment. In reality, it was not merely colder than fifty below
zero; it was colder than sixty below, than seventy below. It was
seventy-five below zero. . . . The dog did not know anything about
thermometers. . . . But the brute had its instinct. It experienced a
vague but menacing apprehension that subdued it and made it slink
along at the man's heels, and that made it question eagerly every
unwonted movement of the man as if expecting him to go into camp
or to seek shelter somewhere and build a fire. (67–68)

Also in keeping with the tragic mode is the sense of inevi-
tability in the catastrophe which must befall the hero. Even
when he builds his first fire for lunch, we know that the reprieve
is temporary: "For the moment the cold of space was out-
witted" (76). There is no doubt in our suspense, only a dreadful
waiting for the disaster. "And then it happened" (78): the curt
announcement is almost a relief. Still, knowing the cruel irony
of the gods, we sense that although the man must surely die,

he will first be mocked in his delusion of security. The man himself does not know this of course, but he does know the gravity of his situation. Having broken through the snow crust over a hidden spring and having wet his legs halfway to the knees, he realizes he must immediately build a fire: "He knew there must be no failure. When it is seventy-five below zero, a man must not fail in his first attempt to build a fire—that is, if his feet are wet. If his feet are dry, and he fails, he can run along the trail for half a mile and restore his circulation. But the circulation of wet and freezing feet cannot be restored by running when it is seventy-five below. No matter how fast he runs, the feet will freeze the harder" (79-80).

The man is fully cognizant of these facts, for they have been told him by the sourdoughs, yet he remains obtuse to their significance. "The cold of space smote the unprotected tip of the planet, and he, being on that unprotected tip, received the full force of the blow. The blood of his body recoiled before it. The blood was alive, like the dog, and like the dog it wanted to hide away and cover itself up from the fearful cold" (80). But the man, working rationally and carefully, manages to build his fire and believes himself safe: "He remembered the advice of the old-timer on Sulphur Creek and smiled. The old-timer had been very serious in laying down the law that no man must travel alone in the Klondike after fifty below. Well, here he was; he had had the accident; he was alone; and he had saved himself. Those old-timers were rather womanish, some of them, he thought. All a man had to do was to keep his head, and he was all right" (81). The irony is dramatic as well as tragic.

"Tragedy," according to Aristotle, "is a representation of an action that is not only complete but that consists of events inspiring fear and pity; and this effect is best produced when the events are at once unexpected and causally related."[19] Moreover, the greatest tragedies are complex: the catastrophe is attended by a sudden reversal in the hero's situation to its opposite and by a discovery, or a change from ignorance to knowledge (303-04); and "of all discoveries the best is that which arises from the action itself, where the shock of surprise is the outcome of a plausible succession of events" (312).

Being human and therefore fallible, London's protagonist

makes a simple, human mistake: he builds his fire under a large, snow-laden spruce tree; and the heat precipitates a small avalanche that blots out the fresh blaze. Reversal and discovery are virtually simultaneous: "The man was shocked. It was as though he had just heard his own sentence of death. For a moment he sat and stared at the spot where the fire had been. Then he grew very calm. Perhaps the old-timer on Sulphur Creek was right. If he had only had a trail-mate he would have been in no danger now. The trail-mate could have built the fire" (83-84).

From this dramatic climax, the story moves through a brilliant dénouement toward its inescapable conclusion. Fighting off panic, the man tries vainly to build another fire; but his fingers are already dead from the cold. Next, he tries ineffectually to kill the dog, thinking he can warm his hands in its body. Then, panic-stricken, he tries running on his frozen feet until he falls exhausted into the snow. Finally, he grows calm and decides to meet death with dignity: "His idea of it was that he had been making a fool of himself, running around like a chicken with its head cut off. . . . Well, he was bound to freeze anyway, and he might as well take it decently. . . . There were lots worse ways to die" (96). In thus resigning himself to his fate, the man achieves true heroic stature; and his tragic action inspires both pity and fear in leading his audience toward the cathartic relief prescribed by Aristotle.

"You were right, old hoss; you were right," the man mumbled to the old-timer of Sulphur Creek.
Then the man drowsed off into what seemed to him the most comfortable and satisfying sleep he had ever known. The dog sat facing him and waiting. The brief day drew to a close in a long, slow twilight. There were no signs of a fire to be made, and, besides, never in the dog's experience had it known a man to sit like that in the snow and make no fire. . . . A little longer it delayed, howling under the stars that leaped and danced and shone brightly in the cold sky. Then it turned and trotted up the trail in the direction of the camp it knew, where were the other food-providers and fire-providers. (97–98)

With this concluding image the tone of the action has been transmuted from dramatic irony into cosmic irony. Gazing at the cold mockery of the heavens, we sense that we are not on the side of the gods and that the man's frailty is also ours. Such is the effect of London's artistry that few of us finish "To Build a Fire" without a subtle shiver of relief to be—at least for the moment—among the "food-providers and fire-providers."

"To Build a Fire" has established itself as a world classic, and while it is instructive to see how much of Aristotle's formula is dramatically reflected in this remarkable work of short fiction, we should realize that the story's greatness does not depend on this formal coincidence and that London himself was probably unaware of these nice parallels with Greek tragedy. The story is great because it derives its informing power from the common mystery that animates the plays of Sophocles and Aeschylus —and all great tragedians—and because it has articulated this mystery with such force that we become mutual participants in the celebration of what Joseph Conrad called "the unavoidable solidarity" of our human destiny. The ultimate source of tragedy is, as Herbert Muller points out, the simple fact that man must die; the great wonder is that, being the one animal who knows this fact, man is still capable of achieving dignity. So long as he possesses this heroic capability, "all is not vanity."[20]

V *Longer Fictions*

That people succumb to these eternal images is an entirely normal matter. It is for this very purpose that the images came into being. They are intended to attract, to convince, and overpower.
—C. G. Jung, *The Integration of the Personality*

In the late summer of 1900 Jack wrote to Cloudesley Johns, "Am winding up the first chapter of novel. Since it is my first attempt, I have chosen a simple subject and shall simply endeavor to make it true, artistic, and interesting" (*Book of Jack London,* I, 345). Five months later, he wrote, "Well, I am on the home stretch of the novel, and it is a failure" (I, 351). The novel, *A Daughter of the Snows*, published in October, 1902, by J. B. Lippincott, was indeed a failure: it is neither true, nor artistic, nor very interesting. C. C. Walcutt has said that the novel is "lavishly prodigal of ideas,"[21] and this lavishness is largely the reason for its failure. "Lord, Lord," Jack sighed, looking back

on it; "how I squandered into it enough stuff for a dozen novels!"
(*Book of Jack London*, I, 384). This work is a potpourri of his
pet ideas on social Darwinism, Anglo-Saxon supremacy, environmentalism, and joy-through-fitness:

Competition was the secret of creation. Battle was the law and
the way of progress. The world was made for the strong, and only
the strong inherited it, and through it there ran an eternal equity.
To be honest was to be strong. To sin was to weaken. . . . "We are
a race of doers and fighters, of globe-encirclers and zone-conquerors.
. . . All that the other races are not, the Anglo-Saxon, or Teuton if
you please, is." . . . Where nature shows the rough hand, the sons
of men are apt to respond with kindred roughness. The amenities
of life spring up only in mellow lands, where the sun is warm and
the earth fat. . . . Thus, in the young Northland, frosty and grim
and menacing, men stripped off the sloth of the south and gave
battle greatly. . . . "Oh, I can swing clubs, and box, and fence," she
cried, successively striking the typical postures; "and swim, and
make high dives, chin a bar twenty times, and—and walk on my
hands. There!" . . . The flush of morning was in her cheek, and its
fire in her eyes, and she was aglow with youth and love. . . . For she
had nursed at the breast of nature. . . .[22]

So preoccupied is the author with ideology that he confuses
fiction with essay. Consequently, ideas assume precedence over
characterization. "The great defect of the novel of ideas," says
Aldous Huxley's Philip Quarles in *Point Counter Point*, "is that
it's a made-up affair. Necessarily; for people who can reel off
neatly formulated notions aren't quite real; they're slightly
monstrous. Living with monsters becomes rather tiresome in
the long run." Old Jacob Welse, the Klondike robber baron
with his Spencer-Carnegie rationalizations; Vance Corliss, the
Yale sissy who gets the girl after reverting atavistically to the
he-manhood of his forebears; Gregory St. Vincent, the smooth-
talking lady's man who turns graceless under pressure; and, above
all, the astonishing Frona Welse, who, we are supposed to believe, captivates every male in the Yukon Territory with her
feminine charm, even while flexing her biceps, spouting the
doctrines of racist imperialism, and bragging that she can do
twenty pull-ups! Such characters do, indeed, "become rather
tiresome in the long run."

London claimed afterward that he had learned a great deal about writing novels from the mistakes he had made in *A Daughter of the Snows,* but the simple truth is that he was a born sprinter who never acquired the artistic stamina of the long-distance runner. The basic technical weaknesses revealed in his first novel were chronic: his longer plots tend to be episodic and disjointed; his dialogue is strained; and his characters often degenerate into caricatures because they are stretched flat on ideological frames. London asserted, "I will sacrifice form *every time,* when it boils down to a final question of choice between form and matter. The thought is the thing." But he did not realize that the literary artist has no such option. It was extremely difficult for him to articulate the larger structures of the novel without some doctrinal meddling such as we find in *Martin Eden, The Valley of the Moon,* and *The Mutiny of the Elsinore;* and, incredible as it seems, his last attempt at writing a novel—*Hearts of Three*—ended in worse failure than his first.[23]

Neither of London's two most successful works of long fiction is a conventional novel: *The Call of the Wild* is a mythic romance; *White Fang,* a sociological fable. Both works are, of course, beast fables in that they provoke our interest—unconsciously if not consciously—in the human situation, not in the plight of the lower animals.[24] By using canine rather than human protagonists, London was able to say more about this situation than he might have been otherwise permitted by the editors of magazines like *The Saturday Evening Post* and *Cosmopolitan* who were extremely careful not to offend the genteel sensibilities of their Victorian readership. Just as two generations earlier Poe had muffled sexual aberrations under the dark mantle of Gothicism, so London hid sex under a heavy cloak of fur as in the vivid scene of "love-making in the Wild, the sex-tragedy of the natural world" in the early pages of *White Fang* when old One Eye and the ambitious young wolf fight to the death while "the she-wolf, the cause of it all," sits and watches with sadistic pleasure. And we also have the example of Buck's ethical retrogression in *The Call of the Wild*: his learning to steal and rob without scruple and to kill without pity does not morally offend us because he is just a dog, not a human.[25]

Full appreciation of *The Call of the Wild* and *White Fang*
begins with "Bâtard," London's first dog story, published in the
June, 1902, issue of *Cosmopolitan* under the euphemistic title
"Diable—A Dog." Although its thematic relationship to the two
later works is inverse, this fine tale shares with both of them
the characteristics of fable and, especially with *White Fang*, the
theme of hereditary and environmental determinism. "Bâtard" is
an anatomy of hatred, and its canine protagonist—"Hell's Spawn,"
as he is called by some—is the antithesis of everything that man's
best friend is supposed to be. It is clear that such devils are not
merely born; they are also made:

> Bâtard did not know his father—hence his name—but, as John Hamlin
> [the storekeeper of the Sixty Mile Post] knew, his father was a
> great gray timber wolf. But the mother of Bâtard, as he dimly re-
> membered her, was a snarling, bickering, obscene husky, full-fronted
> and heavy-chested, with a malign eye, a cat-like grip on life, and
> a genius for trickery and evil. . . . Much of evil and much of strength
> were there in these, Bâtard's progenitors, and, bone and flesh of
> their bone and flesh, he had inherited it all. And then came Black
> Leclère, to lay his heavy hand on the bit of pulsating puppy life,
> to press and prod and mould till it became a big bristling beast,
> acute in knavery, overspilling with hate, sinister, malignant, diabolical.
> With a proper master Bâtard might have made an ordinary, fairly
> efficient sled-dog. He never got the chance: Leclère but confirmed
> him in his congenital iniquity.[26]

His sadistic treatment at the hand of his human antagonist,
the dissolute voyageur, finally transforms Bâtard into the incarnation of evil. Half-starved, tortured, beaten, and cursed, the
dog grows progressively more vicious and cunning—yet he
refuses to leave his master, because he bides with uncanny
patience his time for revenge. Nor can Black Leclère resist
his compulsion to cultivate this hatred. Even after Bâtard has
attacked him in his sleep and has slit his throat, he refuses to
accept the advice of old-timers who urge him to let them shoot
the dog. Leclère, no match for the preternatural malevolence
he has unleashed, is hoisted on his own petard. Near the end of
the story, unjustly convicted of murdering a gold miner, he is
forced to mount a large box, hands tied and noose around his

neck. He gets a last-minute reprieve, but the miners leave him alone—standing precariously on the box—to meditate upon his sinful ways while they go downriver to apprehend the real murderer. When the miners have gone, the dog, grinning, "with a fiendish levity in his bearing that Leclère [cannot] mistake," casually retreats a few yards—then hurls himself against the box on which his helpless master is standing. "Fifteen minutes later, Slackwater Charley and Webster Shaw, returning, caught a glimpse of a ghostly pendulum swinging back and forth in the dim light. As they hurriedly drew in closer, they made out the man's inert body, and a live thing that clung to it, and shook and worried, and gave to it the swaying motion" (231).

London said he wrote *The Call of the Wild* to redeem the species. "I started it as a companion to my other dog-story 'Batard,' which you may remember; but it got away from me, and instead of 4000 words it ran 32000 before I could call a halt" (*Book of Jack London,* I, 388). Joan London tells us that so far as her father was concerned, this masterpiece was "a purely fortuitous piece of work, a lucky shot in the dark that had unexpectedly found its mark," and that, when reviewers enthusiastically interpreted *The Call of the Wild* as a brilliant human allegory, he was astonished: "'I plead guilty,' he admitted, 'but I was unconscious of it at the time. I did not mean to do it.'"[27] However, he was not entirely oblivious to the story's unusual merit; in a letter to his publisher George Brett, he wrote: "It is an animal story, utterly different in subject and treatment from the rest of the animal stories which have been so successful; and yet it seems popular enough for the 'Saturday Evening Post,' for they snapped it up right away."[28]

Though London may not have understood the full import of this statement, his story was in fact "utterly different" from the humanized beasts in Kipling's "Mowgli" stories and from the sentimental projections of Margaret Marshall Saunders's *Beautiful Joe* and Ernest Seton's *Biography of a Grizzly,* which were enormously popular in London's day and which can still be found in the children's sections of public libraries. Charles G. D. Roberts, writing about the appeal of such literature at the turn of the century, explained that "the animal story, as we now have it, is a potent emancipator. It frees us for a little while from

the world of shop-worn utilities, and from the mean tenement
of self of which we do well to grow weary.... It has ever the
more significance, it has ever the richer gift of refreshment and
renewal, the more humane the heart and spiritual the understanding which we bring to the intimacy of it."[29] This explanation holds true for *The Call of the Wild* as well as for the other
wild animal stories: London's work offers the "gift of refreshment and renewal," as well as a certain escapism. The difference
is its radical departure from the conventional animal story in
style and substance—the manner in which it is, to use the psycho-
analytic term, "overdetermined" in its multilayered meaning.[30]

Maxwell Geismar gives a clue to the deeper layer of meaning when he classifies the work as "a beautiful prose poem, or
nouvelle, of gold and death on the instinctual level" and as a
"handsome parable of the buried impulses."[31] We need only
interpolate that these "buried impulses" are essentially human,
not canine, and that the reader identifies more closely than he
realizes with the protagonist of that *nouvelle*. The plot is animated by one of the most basic of archetypal motifs: the Myth
of the Hero. The call to adventure, departure, initiation, the
perilous journey to the "world navel" or mysterious life-center,
transformation, and apotheosis—these are the phases of the Myth;
and all are present in Buck's progress from the civilized world
through the natural and beyond to the supernatural world.[32]
His journey carries him not only through space but also through
time and, ultimately, into the still center of a world that is
timeless.

Richard Chase points out that in the type of long fiction most
properly designated as the *romance*, character becomes "somewhat abstract and ideal," and plot is "highly colored": "Astonishing events may occur, and these are likely to have a symbolic
or ideological, rather than a realistic, plausibility. Being less
committed to the immediate rendition of reality than the novel,
the romance will more freely veer toward mythic, allegorical,
and symbolistic forms."[33] All of these remarks are directly
applicable to *The Call of the Wild*, in which the richly symbolistic
form ultimately becomes the content of the fiction. The seven
chapters of the work fall into four major parts or movements.
Each of these movements is distinguished by its own theme,

rhythm, and tone; each is climaxed by an event of dramatic intensity; and each marks a stage in the hero's transformation from a phenomenal into an ideal figure.

Part I, consisting of three chapters, is, with its emphasis on physical violence and amoral survival, the most Naturalistic— and the most literal—of the book. Its rhythms are quick, fierce, muscular. Images of intense struggle, pain, and blood predominate. Chapter I, "Into the Primitive," describes the great dog's kidnapping from Judge Miller's pastoral ranch and his subsequent endurance of the first rites of his initiation—the beginning of the transformation that ultimately carries him deep into Nature's heart of darkness: "For two days and nights he neither ate nor drank, and during those two days and nights of torment, he accumulated a fund of wrath that boded ill for whoever first fell foul of him. His eyes turned blood-shot, and he was metamorphosed into a raging fiend. So changed was he that the Judge himself would not have recognized him; and the express messengers breathed with relief when they bundled him off the train at Seattle."[34]

The high priest of Buck's first initiatory rites is the symbolic figure in the red sweater, the man with the club who relentlessly pounds the hero into a disciplined submission to the code of violence and toil. "Well, Buck, my boy," the man calmly observes after the merciless beating, "we've had our little ruction, and the best thing we can do is to let it go at that. You've learned your place, and I know mine" (32). Like all of London's heroes who survive the rigors of the White Silence, Buck has passed the first test: that of adaptability.

Chapter II, "The Law of Club and Fang," takes the hero to the Northland. On the Dyea beach he encounters the dogs and men who are to become his traveling companions in the long hard months ahead. He also continues to absorb the lessons of survival. Curly, the most amiable of the newly arrived pack, is knocked down by a veteran husky, then ripped apart by the horde of canine spectators. The scene remains vividly etched in Buck's memory: "So that was the way. No fairplay. Once down, that was the end of you" (45). Later, as he is broken into his traces for the trail, he awakens to the great driving motivation of the veteran sled-dogs: the extraordinary love of toil. But

more significant is the metamorphosis of his moral values. He
learns, for example, that stealing, an unthinkable misdeed in his
former state, can be the difference between survival and death:

[His] first theft marked Buck as fit to survive in the hostile Northland
environment. It marked his adaptability, his capacity to adjust himself
to changing conditions, the lack of which would have meant swift
and terrible death. It marked, further, the decay or going to pieces
of his moral nature, a vain thing and a handicap in the ruthless
struggle for existence. It was all well enough in the Southland, under
the law of love and fellowship, to respect private property and
personal feelings; but in the Northland, under the law of club and
fang, whoso took such things into account was a fool, and in so far
as he observed them he would fail to prosper. (59–60)

Chapter III, "The Dominant Primordial Beast," marks the conclusion of the first major phase of Buck's initiation; for it reveals
that he is not merely qualified as a member of the pack but
that he is worthy of leadership. In this chapter, there is a pro-
nounced modulation of style to signal the glimmerings of Buck's
mythic destiny; instead of sharply detailed physical description,
we begin to encounter passages of tone-poetry:

With the aurora borealis flaming coldly overhead, or the stars leaping
in the frost dance, and the land numb and frozen under its pall of
snow, this song of the huskies might have been the defiance of life,
only it was pitched in minor key, with long-drawn wailings and
half-sobs, and was more the pleading of life, the articulate travail
of existence. . . . When he moaned and sobbed, it was with the pain
of living that was of old the pain of his wild fathers, and the fear
and mystery of the cold and dark that was to them fear and
mystery. (84–87)

London's style becomes increasingly lyrical as the narrative
rises from literal to symbolic level, and it reaches such intensity
near the end of Chapter III that we now realize that Buck's is no
common animal story:

There is an ecstasy that marks the summit of life, and beyond which
life cannot rise. And such is the paradox of living, this ecstasy comes
when one is most alive, and it comes as a complete forgetfulness that

one is alive. This ecstasy, this forgetfulness of living, comes to the artist, caught up and out of himself in a sheet of flame; it comes to the soldier, war-mad on a stricken field and refusing quarter; and it came to Buck, leading the pack, sounding the old wolf-cry, straining after the food that was alive and that fled swiftly before him through the moonlight. He was sounding the deeps of his nature, and of the parts of his nature that were deeper than he, going back into the womb of Time. He was mastered by the sheer surging of life, the tidal wave of being, the perfect joy of each separate muscle, joint, and sinew in that it was everything that was not death, that it was aglow and rampant, expressing itself in movement, flying exultantly under the stars and over the face of dead matter that did not move. (91)

This paragraph is a thematic epitome of the whole work, and it functions as a prologue to the weird moonlit scene in which Buck challenges Spitz for leadership of the team, a scene noted by Geismar as "a perfect instance of the 'son-horde' theory which Frazer traced in *The Golden Bough*, and of that primitive ritual to which Freud himself attributed both a sense of original sin and the fundamental ceremony of religious exorcism" (*Rebels and Ancestors*, 150-51).

Even though Buck has now "Won to Mastership" (Chapter IV), he is not ready for apotheosis; he is a leader and a hero— but he is not yet a god. His divinity must be confirmed, as prescribed by ritual, through death and rebirth. After the climactic pulsations of Chapter III, there is a slowing of beat in the second movement. Death occurs symbolically, almost literally, in Chapter V ("The Toil of Trace and Trail"). Clustering darkly, the dominant images are those of pain and fatigue as Buck and his teammates suffer under the ownership of the three *chechaquos*: Charles, his wife Mercedes, and her brother Hal— "a nice family party." Like the two Incapables of "In a Far Country," they display all the fatal symptoms of incompetence and unfitness: "Buck felt vaguely that there was no depending upon these two men and the woman. They did not know how to do anything, and as days went by it became apparent that they could not learn. They were slack in all things, without order or discipline" (138). Without a sense of economy or the will to work and endure hardship themselves, they overwork, starve, and beat their dogs—then they turn on one another: "Their irritability arose out of their misery, increased with it, doubled upon it, outdistanced it. The wonderful patience of the trail which comes to all men who toil hard and suffer sore, and remain sweet of speech and kindly, did not come to these two men and the woman. They had no inkling of such a patience. They were stiff and in pain; their muscles ached, their bones ached, their very hearts ached; and because of this they became sharp of speech, and hard words were first on their lips in the morning and last at night" (141). This ordeal is the second long and difficult phase of Buck's initiation. The "long journey" is described in increasingly morbid imagery as the "perambulating skeletons" and "wayfarers of death" approach closer to their fatal end in the thawing ice of Yukon River; the journey ends with Buck's symbolic crucifixion as he is beaten nearly to death by Hal shortly before the ghostly caravan moves on without him and disappears into the lethal river.

Buck's rebirth comes in Chapter VI, "For the Love of a Man," which also functions as the third and transitional movement of the narrative. Having been rescued by John Thornton, the benign helper who traditionally appears in the Myth to lead the hero toward his goal, Buck is now being readied for the final phase of his odyssey. Appropriately, the season is spring; and the mood is idyllic as he wins back his strength, "lying by the river bank through the long spring days, watching the running water, listening lazily to the songs of the birds and the hum of nature..." (161). And, during this same convalescent period, the hints of his destiny grow more insistent: "He was older than the days he had seen and the breaths he had drawn. He linked the past with the present, and the eternity behind him throbbed through him in a mighty rhythm to which he swayed as the tides and seasons swayed.... Deep in the forest a call was sounding.... But as often as he gained the soft unbroken earth and the green shade, the love for John Thornton drew him back..." (168-71). The passionate devotion to Thornton climaxes in the final scene of Chapter VI when Buck wins a thousand-dollar wager for his master by moving a half-ton sled a hundred yards; this legendary feat, which concludes the third movement of the narrative, foreshadows the hero's supernatural appointment in the fourth and final movement.

Chapter VII, "The Sounding of the Call," consummates Buck's transformation. In keeping with this change, London shifts both the setting and the tone. Thornton, taking the money earned by Buck in the wager, begins his last quest "into the East after a fabled lost mine, the history of which was as old as the history of the country . . . steeped in tragedy and shrouded in mystery." As the small party moves into the wilderness, the scene assumes a mythic atmosphere and the caravan is enveloped in a strange aura of timelessness:

> The months came and went, and back and forth they twisted through the uncharted vastness, where no men were and yet where men had been if the Lost Cabin were true. They went across divides in summer blizzards, shivered under the midnight sun on naked mountains between the timber line and the eternal snows, dropped into summer valleys amid swarming gnats and flies, and in the shadows of glaciers picked strawberries and flowers as ripe and fair as any the Southland could boast. In the fall of the year they penetrated a weird lake country, sad and silent, where wild-fowl had been, but where then there was no life nor sign of life—only the blowing of chill winds, the forming of ice in sheltered places, and the melancholy rippling of waves on lonely beaches. (195–96)

The weirdness of the atmosphere is part of the "call to adventure" described by Joseph Campbell in *The Hero with a Thousand Faces,* which "signifies that destiny has summoned the hero and transferred his spiritual center of gravity from within the pale of society to a zone unknown. This fateful region of both treasure and danger may be variously represented: as a distant land, a forest, . . . or profound dream state; but it is always a place of strangely fluid and polymorphous beings, unimaginable torments, superhuman deeds and impossible delight" (58). This "fateful region of both treasure and danger" is a far cry from Judge Miller's pastoral ranch and from the raw frontier of the Klondike gold rush: it is the landscape of myth. The party finally arrives at its destination, a mysterious and incredibly rich placer-valley where "Like giants they toiled, days flashing on the heels of days like dreams as they heaped the treasure up" (197).

His role fulfilled as guide into the unknown zone to the

"World Navel," Thornton and his party are killed by the savage
Yeehats; and Buck is released from the bond of love to fulfill
the last phase of his apotheosis as he is transformed into the
immortal Ghost Dog of Northland legend; he incarnates the
eternal mystery of creation and life: "[And when] the long
winter nights come on and the wolves follow their meat into
the lower valleys . . . a great, gloriously coated wolf, like, and
yet unlike, all other wolves . . . may be seen running at the head
of the pack through the pale moonlight or glimmering borealis,
leaping gigantic above his fellows, his great throat abellow as he
sings a song of the younger world, which is the song of the
pack" (228-31).

Though *The Call of the Wild* was perhaps no luckier than
any other great artistic achievement, it was "a shot in the dark"
in an unintended sense—into the dark wilderness of the unconscious. And as with other great literary works, its ultimate
meaning eludes us. But at least a significant part of that meaning relates to the area of human experience which cannot be
translated into discursive terms and which must therefore be
approached tentatively and obliquely. After granting this much,
we may infer that the animating force of London's wild romance
is the vital energy Jung called *libido* and that London's hero is
a projection of the reader's own *self* which is eternally striving
for psychic integration in the process called *individuation*. Such
an inference accounts for the appropriateness of London's
division of his narrative into seven chapters which fall naturally
into four movements: quaternity symbolizing, in Jung's words,
"the ideal of completeness" and "the totality of the personality"
—seven, the archetypal number of perfect order and the con-
summation of a cycle.[35] But, of course, we do not need such a
technical explanation to know that the call to which we respond
as the great Ghost Dog flashes through the glimmering borealis
singing his song of the younger world is the faint but clear echo
of a music deep within ourselves.

In 1904, following the immediate success of *The Call of the
Wild*, London wrote to George Brett that he had decided to
compose a "complete antithesis [and] companion-book": ". . . I'm
going to reverse the process. Instead of devolution or deciviliza-
tion of a dog, I'm going to give the evolution, the civilization of

a dog—development of domesticity, faithfulness, love, morality, and all the amenities and virtues" (*Letters from Jack London,* 166). Two years afterwards this "companion-book" was published under the title of *White Fang.* Instead of being a true companion piece, however, *White Fang* is a completely different kind of book from *The Call of the Wild,* clearly illustrating the basic distinctions between Jung's "visionary mode" and "psychological mode." Structured upon ideas rather than upon myth, *White Fang* is a sociological fable intended to illustrate London's theories of environmentalism.

More Naturalistic than *The Call of the Wild,* the opening description of the frozen-hearted Northland is as powerful as anything London ever wrote in this vein. Here he depicts nature as a vast intransigent force utterly hostile to puny, inconsequential men who are "pitting themselves against the might of a world as remote and alien and pulseless as the abyss of space."[36] Unlike the animated Wild to which Buck reverts, this is the wilderness of the White Silence, predicated upon the death-principle: "Life is an offense to it, for life is movement; and the Wild aims always to destroy movement. It freezes the water to prevent it running to the sea; it drives the sap out of the trees till they are frozen to their mighty hearts; and most ferociously and terribly of all does the Wild harry and crush into submission man—man, who is the most restless of life, ever in revolt against the dictum that all movement must in the end come to the cessation of movement" (4-5). Into this forbidding world the young wolf cub is born, and he learns early that life is an eat-or-be-eaten affair and that the forces of life move inexorably toward death in one violent form or another.

Set against this principle and providing the central tension of the work is a cluster of contrasting values: life, love, civilization, the Southland; and toward these the protagonist moves during his rites of passage. In *White Fang,* a proper initiation story, the hero follows the conventional pattern of separation, ordeal, transformation, return, and full integration as a full-fledged, responsible member of society. At the conclusion, White Fang has been transformed by love from a savage beast into a thoroughly domesticated pet: "Not alone was he in the geographical Southland, for he was in the Southland of life. Human kindness was like a sun shining upon him, and he flourished like a flower planted in good soil" (305). From this perspective, *White Fang* may be regarded as a companion piece and antithesis, not to *The Call of the Wild*, but to "Bâtard," in which a misbegotten brute is shaped by maltreatment into a fiend. To make sure the reader perceives the message, the author inserts into the closing pages of *White Fang* the episode of the escaped convict Jim Hall, who is a human version of Bâtard. Hall has been "ill-made in the making," we are told; and the harsh treatment he has received from society, "from the time he was a little pulpy boy in a San Francisco slum—soft clay in the hands of society and ready to be formed into something," has turned him into "so terrible a beast that he can best be characterized as carnivorous" (315-16).

The dramatic confrontation between these two contrasting products of environmental determinism—the brutalized man and the civilized beast—occurs when the escaped convict breaks into Judge Scott's home to "wreak vengeance" on the man who he thinks has "railroaded" him to prison. Jim Hall is a mad dog who must be destroyed for the safety of respectable citizens, but London makes it clear, as he had done in "Bâtard," that the responsibility for such creatures rests squarely on the society that has molded them. As he said to George Wharton James, "I know men and women as they are—millions of them yet in the slime stage. But I am an evolutionist, therefore a broad optimist, hence my love for the human (in the slime though he be) comes from my knowing him as he is and seeing the divine possibilities ahead of him. That's the whole motive of my 'White Fang.' Every atom of organic life is plastic. The finest specimens now in existence were once all pulpy infants capable of being moulded this way or that. Let the pressure be one way and we have atavism—the reversion to the wild; the other the domestication, civilization. I have always been impressed with the awful plasticity of life and I feel that I can never lay enough stress upon the marvelous power and influence of environment."[37]

White Fang is an effective dramatization of this theme and continues to be widely read, but from the artistic viewpoint it is less impressive than *The Call of the Wild* because it is written in what Eliseo Vivas has called the "transitive" mode: its function is to point toward the cognitive and the moral. *The Call of the Wild* is, on the other hand, purely esthetic and intransitive: it engages the reader in a rapt attention for no other purpose than the unique experience of art.[38] Rather than pointing outward to society, *The Call of the Wild* points inward to something marvelous within man—the everlasting mystery of life itself.

The artistic significance of *The Call of the Wild* was recognized at once in one of those rare instances when critical taste and popular appetite agree, and Jack London was acclaimed by the world as a major writer. During the years afterward, he had other moments of "primordial" inspiration, but none surpassed the sustained vision of this extraordinary "parable of the buried impulses."

CHAPTER 3

Success

> Why certes, if they wish to buy me, body and soul, they are welcome—if they pay the price. I am writing for money; if I can procure fame, that means more money. More money means more life to me.
> —Jack London, letter to Cloudesley Johns (1900)

> As a brain merchant I was a success. Society opened its portals to me. I entered right in on the parlor floor, and my disillusionment proceeded rapidly.
> —Jack London, "What Life Means to Me" (1906)

JACK London made no bones about his reasons for writing. "If cash comes with fame, come fame," he wrote to his friend Johns; "if cash comes without fame, come cash" (*Letters from Jack London,* 71). But it was not the money itself or the making of the money that he really wanted; he wanted what the money would buy: "I shall always hate the task of getting money," he confessed in 1900; "every time I sit down to write it is with great disgust. I'd sooner be out in the open wandering around most any old place. So the habit of money-getting will never become one of my vices. But the habit of money spending, ah God! I shall always be its victim" (*Letters from Jack London,* 96-97). There is some truth in Granville Hicks's remark that "In his attitude towards money London was indistinguishable from any middle-class man on the make,"[1] but it is the kind of partial truth often conveyed through condescension: in ignoring the larger implications, it risks missing the point entirely.

The point is that London was forever playing the role of the American Adam. As in the case of Fitzgerald's famous Gatsby —and London's own Martin Eden—the obsession to get money was materialistic and vulgar only in the most superficial way; fundamentally, the conception was ideal. In this ideal sense, money—though essential—was the means to an end, never an end in itself. The concept was part of the old American Dream again, older than Ben Franklin, who popularized this myth derived from the Puritan ethic: material gain was a sign of spiritual grace; through His special providences, the Almighty smiled visibly upon His saints by rewarding their labors with profit in the affairs of this world. Older than the Puritans, material gain was inextricable from man's age-old dream for the better life. Money was in truth the coin of the New Realm, for would it not buy happiness, esteem, the richer life? "More money means more life to me," said London; and this statement was a key to his meteoric career, just as it is a key to the larger Dream.

I *Portrait of the Artist as a Professional*

Sincerity was the greatest trait of [Jack London's] character. He never made pretensions and he built neither his work nor his life on sophisms and evasions.   —Anna Strunsky Walling[2]

Jack London's open confession—or boast—that his motives were commercial has provided modern critics with a handy excuse for consigning both him and his work to the literary dustbin. Their reasoning is something like this: (1) *fact*—London is not highly regarded by today's most prestigious critics (*assumption*—the contemporary critical eye is clear and far-seeing); (2) *fact*—he was, and remains in some lower circles, exceedingly popular (*assumption*—popularity is in league with vulgarity, artistic cheapness, and ephemerality); and (3) *fact*—he admitted that he wrote for cash, insisting that he hated writing and had little regard for what he had written (*assumption*—the worthy author is above all a dedicated artist for whom mundane things are of secondary importance); *therefore,* he must be a hack and, at best, "an interesting sideshow in the naturalist carnival";[3] but he is hardly deserving of serious critical attention.

The facts are indisputably true, but the faulty assumptions lead to the wrong conclusion. First, the notorious case of Herman Melville, whose great work was ignored by two generations of

critics, persuasively demonstrates the tenuous correlation between literary merit and critical acclaim. The critic's vision,
collectively as well as individually, is often astigmatic and sometimes myopic.

Second, the example of Mark Twain indicates that, notwithstanding the significant influence of Arnold Bennett's "passionate few," the plain taste of the masses may occasionally prevail
if the writer has tapped the wellsprings of myth and folk
culture. Furthermore, as the British critic Winifred Blatchford
has written, "Jack London is known as a 'popular' writer, and
certainly he is more greatly read by all classes of readers than
are most writers. But his popularity was not gained by cheapness, as is usually the case. He had a great public not because
he wrote down to the public, but because what he wrote was
always intensely alive and understandable."[4]

Third, with regard to London's mercenary taint, we might
recall Dr. Johnson's quip that "No man but a blockhead ever
wrote except for money." Admittedly, we beg the question with
this quotation; nevertheless, a fair assessment of London's
artistic integrity must begin with the recognition that his attitude
toward writing was thoroughly professional—that is, he deliberately chose writing as the sole means of making his livelihood;
he underwent rigorous training to acquire the special expertise
of his chosen field; he wrote with the full expectation of being
paid well for his investment; he maintained the discipline of
steady application of his time and energies to his vocation; and,
once having become secure in his accomplished skill, he regarded it with a confidence bordering on contempt. At the same
time, his work was generally governed by a clear-cut professional
code comprising an ethic, a mystique, and a practical esthetic.

The ethic was sincerity. In 1907, reacting to the suggestion
by Macmillan's George P. Brett that publication of his disrep-
utable tramping experiences might damage the sales of his
other works, London asserted: "In *The Road,* and in all my work,
in all that I have said and written and done, I have been true.
This is the character I have built up; it constitutes, I believe, my
big asset.... I have always insisted that the cardinal literary
virtue is sincerity, and I have striven to live up to this belief"
(*Letters from Jack London,* 241). Earlier, he prescribed for

aspiring young writers: "The three great things are: GOOD
HEALTH; WORK; and a PHILOSOPHY OF LIFE. I may add,
nay, must add, a fourth—SINCERITY. Without this, the other
three are without avail; with it you may cleave to greatness and
sit among giants."[5] To be candid was to tell the truth as he
saw it in relationship to his philosophy of life; it was to be true
to his artistic self as that self had been shaped by experience;
and it meant that he must in his fiction articulate the basic,
cosmic realities.

The mystique was imaginative Realism or, as London phrased
it in *Martin Eden,* "an impassioned realism, shot through with
human aspiration and faith.... life as it [is], with all its spirit-
groping and soul-reaching left in," a truthful compromise between "the school of god" and "the school of clod," charged
with vitality and with "humanness." The impassioned Realist
"must seize upon and press into enduring art-forms the vital facts
of our existence." And, while he will always endeavor to fuse
his Realism with imaginative beauty and with the true spirit
of romance and adventure, he must never shun the terrible and
the tragic in favor of the illusion of life's "sweet commonplaces."
The sincere writer will be as forceful as he is honest—for "what
more is the function of art than to excite states of consciousness
complementary to the thing portrayed? The color of tragedy
must be red." In sum, the supreme fiction will be truer than
phenomenal reality because the writer's imagination will have
seized upon the cosmic essence, thereby making it "LIVE, and
spout blood and spirit and beauty and fire and glamor."[6]

London's esthetic, informed by the same vital honesty, manifested itself in functionalism: "Art, to be truly effective, should
be part and parcel of life and pervade it in all its interstices."[7]
Only so much beauty does an object possess as it has utility:
"What finer beauty than strength—whether it be airy steel, or
massive masonry, or a woman's hand? ... A thing must be true,
or it is not beautiful, any more than a painted wanton is beautiful, any more than a sky-scraper is beautiful that is intrinsically
and structurally light and that has a false massiveness of pillars
plastered on outside."[8] In writing, then, vigorous content is
essential: "What the world wants is strength of utterance, not
precision of utterance.... the person who would be precise is

merely an echo of all the precise people who have gone before, and such a person's work is bound to be colorless and insipid" (*Book of Jack London*, II, 11). "What is form?" London demanded in a letter to Elwyn Hoffman; "What intrinsic value resides in it? None, none, none—unless it clothe pregnant substance, great substance."[9] Granting that language is merely the vehicle for thought, the honest writer will therefore eschew decorative prose and strive to develop a style "not only concentrative, compact, but crisp, incisive, terse."[10] Praising Spencer's "Philosophy of Style," London wrote:

It taught me to transmute thought, beauty, sensation and emotion into black symbols on white paper; which symbols, through the reader's eye, were taken into his brain, and by his brain transmuted into thoughts, beauty, sensations and emotions that fairly corresponded with mine. Among other things, this taught me to know the brain of my reader, in order to select the symbols that would compel his brain to realize my thought, or vision, or emotion. Also, I learned that the right symbols were the ones that would require the expenditure of the minimum of my reader's brain energy, leaving the maximum of his brain energy to realize and enjoy the content of my mind, as conveyed to his mind.   (*Book of Jack London*, II, 50)

Simplistic as such comments seem by late twentieth-century critical standards, London was fully representative of his own age when he remarked that "It tolerates Mr. [Henry] James, but it prefers Mr. Kipling";[11] and he was well in advance of that age when he asserted that "there is no utility that need not be beautiful" and that "construction and decoration must be one."[12]

Because London discovered early in his career that writing fiction paid better than writing literary criticism, he published relatively few essays on the art of fiction; but the many letters of advice he so generously wrote, along with the handful of his critical essays, reveal his mastery of his craft. Dissimilar though the two appear to be in so many ways, London would have agreed with Henry James that the absolute requirement for a work of fiction is that it must be interesting and that the quality of the work of art is directly proportional to the quality of the mind of the producer: "You must have your hand on the inner pulse of things," he admonished the young writer; "the very form of the thinking is the expression. . . . if your expression is poor, it is because your thought is poor, if narrow, because you are narrow."[13] He would have agreed, moreover, with James's concept of experience as a state of mind; their difference was that for James artistic sensibility was an exquisite silken web but for London it was a trawling net. Yet in both cases the supreme virtue was the illusion of life conveyed through the artistic transaction. Long before T. S. Eliot circulated his "objective correlative," Jack advised Cloudesley Johns, "Don't you tell the reader. [INSTEAD,] HAVE YOUR CHARACTERS TELL IT BY THEIR DEEDS, ACTIONS, TALK, ETC. Then, and not until then, are you writing fiction and not a sociological paper.... Atmosphere stands always for the elimination of the artist, that is to say, the atmosphere is the artist..." (*Letters from Jack London*, 108).

The most thorough exposition of London's attitude toward the artist as a professional craftsman is found in his early article "First Aid to Rising Authors," first published in the December, 1900, issue of *Junior Munsey Magazine* and posthumously reprinted as "The Material Side" in *The Occident*. In this seminal essay London divides writers into two major categories. The first group consists of those for whom writing is a part-time, secondary activity: (1) the specialist—the doctor, the lawyer, the professor, the scientist—who writes in order to disseminate the knowledge of his profession; (2) the social gadfly who writes merely to get his name into print; and (3) the literary dabbler or dilettante who writes for the same reason he hunts, travels, or attends the opera—for diversion and pleasure. The second group are the serious authors for whom writing is a way of life, and these comprise three major types: (1) the true poet "who sings for the song's sake" and "because he cannot help singing"; (2) the didactic "heavenly, fire-flashing, fire-bringing" soul who has —or thinks he has—"a message the world needs or would be glad to hear" and whose "ambition is to teach, to help, to uplift"; and (3) the ambitious, practical man who is driven by "belly need" and by an obsession to achieve the good life. Without compunction Jack places himself in this last group:

... We are joy-loving, pleasure-seeking and we are ever hungry for the things which we deem the compensation of living: ... good food . . . nice houses with sanitary plumbing and tight roofs . . . books, pictures, pianos . . . saddle horses, bicycles, and automobiles; cameras, shot guns, and jointed rods; canoes, catboats, and yawls . . . railroad tickets, tents, and camping outfits. . . . When India starves, or the town needs a library, or the poor man in the neighborhood loses his one horse and falls sick, we want to put our hands in our pockets and help. And to do all this, we want cash!

Because we want these things, . . . we are going to rush into print to get them. . . . We have chosen print because we were better adapted for it; and, further, because we preferred it to pulling teeth, mending broken bones, adding up figures, or working with pick and shovel.

If one chooses to write for cash, he should write the kind of stuff that will pay best; and fiction pays best. Even so, the professional craftsman must exercise some judgment about the kind of fiction he writes; he should avoid "the inanely vapid sort which amuses the commonplace public, and the melodramatic messes which tickle the palates of the sensation mongers. . . . Of course it pays; but . . ."—and here is a key to the paradox of London's view of his work—

. . . because we happen to be mercenarily inclined, there is no reason why we should lose our self-respect. A man material enough of soul to work for his living is not, in consequence, so utterly bad as to be incapable of exercising choice. . . . Though the dreamers and idealists scorn us because of our close contact with the earth, no disgrace need attach to the contact. The flesh may sit heavily upon us, yet may we stand erect and look one another in the eyes.

And in this connection we may well take a lesson from those same dreamers and idealists. Let us be fire-bringers in a humble way. Let us have an eye to the ills of the world and its needs; and if we find messages, let us deliver them. Ah, pardon me, purely for materialistic reasons. We will weave them about with our fictions, and make them beautiful, and sell them for goodly sums.

Of course there is danger in this. It is liable to be catching. We may become possessed by our ideas, and be whisked away into the clouds. But we won't inoculate. Honor bright, we won't inoculate.[14]

The complexity of London's theory of his craft is revealed in these playful ironies. By his own admission he was a commercial artist who wrote from "belly need" and for the material accouterments of the Great Society—but he was also a self-respecting professional. More than this, he was also on occasion a true poet, a dreamer, and an idealist. Finally, he was an ideological "fire-bringer" who wrote a good many messages with a sharper eye to indoctrination than to profit.

II   *Ideological Inoculations*

I love to teach, to transmit to others the ideas and impressions in my own consciousness.   —*Book of Jack London*, II, 45

Porter Garnett, in an early assessment of London's work, wrongly predicted that London would "take his place in the encyclopedias as a philosopher and a propagandist rather than as a literary artist."[15] But his was an understandable error. The amount of London's work written primarily to indoctrinate rather than to sell should easily disprove the accusations that he was a hack. A half-dozen of his books, as the quickest glance at his titles reveals, are overtly propagandistic; and he was fully aware of the unpopularity and, therefore, of the economic risks of his Socialist preachings. Less obvious but no less important is the quantity of his profit-motivated work which is also didactic. Few major fictionists have committed themselves more openly to ideology in so much of their writing, and no American author has been more transparent or, for that matter, less secretive. In his writing London told everything he knew—and unwittingly revealed more than he knew.

His literary collaboration with Anna Strunsky is a case in point. When they met in the fall of 1899 at a lecture by Socialist Austin Lewis, Jack was immediately attracted to the brilliant young liberal: "I shall be over Saturday night," he announced in a letter to her a few days afterward. "If you draw back upon yourself, what have I left? Take me this way: a stray guest, a bird of passage, splashing with salt-rimed wings through a brief moment of your life—a rude and blundering bird, used to large airs and great spaces, unaccustomed to the amenities of confined existence" (*Letters from Jack London*, 77). Reminiscing years later, Anna wrote: "He was youth, adventure, romance. He was a poet and a social revolutionist. He had a genius for friendship. He loved and was greatly beloved."[16]

Yet, despite his great affection for Anna, Jack married Bessie
Maddern the following spring—not because of romantic love but
because he wanted "seven sturdy Saxon sons and seven beautiful daughters."[17] A few months later he rationalized his decision
in an epistolary dialogue with Anna published pseudonymously
by Macmillan in 1903 as *The Kempton-Wace Letters*. As he
wrote to Cloudesley Johns in October, 1900, "Didn't I explain
my volume of letters? Well, it's this way: A young Russian Jewess
of 'Frisco and myself have often quarreled over our concep-
tions of love. She happens to be a genius. She is also a materialist
by philosophy, and an idealist by innate preference, and is constantly being forced to twist all the facts of the universe in
order to reconcile herself with herself. So, finally, we decided
that the only way to argue the question out would be by letter"
(*Letters from Jack London*, 113). The question was argued out,
to be sure, but not in the way Jack had intended; for the ultimate
effect of the debate was to purge him of his rational-scientific
attitude toward love.

"Love is something that begins in sensation and ends in sentiment," he writes behind the persona of a young economics professor named Herbert Wace who is attacking the romantic views
of his older friend Dane Kempton (Miss Strunsky); it is *"a
disorder of mind and body, and is produced by passion under
the stimulus of imagination."*[18] The entire tradition of romantic
love is nothing but "pre-nuptial madness" (89), "an artifice,
blunderingly and unwittingly introduced by man into the natural
order" (170). The deluded romantic lover, unable to reconcile
his carnal passions with his idealized sentiment, agonizes in his
"sense of sin and shame and personal degradation"; for he fails
to realize that "the need for perpetuation is the cause of passion;
and that human passion, working through imagination and
worked upon by imagination, becomes love" (89). This emotion
is simply *"a means for the perpetuation and development of the
human type"* and may be improved through the application of
human reason (67). A sensible marriage "is based upon reason
and service and healthy sacrifice.... In a word, and in the
fullest sense of the word, it is sex comradeship" (69).

Ironically, Jack soon abandoned the tough reasonableness of
his own attitude. As Anna later remarked, "He held that love is

only a trap set by nature for the individual. One must not marry for love but for certain qualities discerned by the mind. This he argued in 'The Kempton-Wace Letters' brilliantly and passionately; so passionately as to again make one suspect that he was not as certain of his position as he claimed to be" (*Book of Jack London*, I, 360). Between the inception and publication of the *Letters*, something happened to change radically London's views about love. At the end of the book, Herbert Wace, smugly rational, is rejected by his fiancée, thereby signifying a victory for Dane Kempton's romantic argument. Apparently the course of Jack's own marriage, which had been predicated on the same thesis argued in the book, had altered his belief that one could successfully marry without passion. Writing to Cloudesley Johns in the late summer of 1903, a few weeks after his separation from Bessie, he drily commented: "It's all right for a man sometimes to marry philosophically, but remember, it's damned hard on the woman" (*Book of Jack London*, I, 398). Two years later, as soon as the divorce was final, he married Charmian Kittredge for romantic love.

On July 21, 1902, a few weeks after London had finished his collaboration with Anna and his proofing of *A Daughter of the Snows*, he received a wire from the American Press Association asking him to go to South Africa to report the aftermath of the Boer War. He left the next day, stopping over in New York to meet with George P. Brett, president of Macmillan, and to discuss publication of *The Kempton-Wace Letters*. During the discussion he also made an agreement to publish a study of conditions in the London slums, which he planned to research during his layover in England. It was a fortunate agreement, for his South African series was cancelled. Despite dire predictions that he would never be seen alive again by his friends, he spent ten shillings at a second-hand clothing shop in Petticoat Lane for a change of wardrobe and, disguised as a stranded and broke American seaman, disappeared into the black heart of the East End. On August 9, he stood in Trafalgar Square indistinguishable from the thousands of derelicts who threw their dirty caps into the air amid shouts of "God save the King!" as Edward VII rode by in his Coronation Day parade.

Jack had endured considerable hardship and had lived close

to poverty most of his life, but nothing in his past experiences compared with what he saw in that "City of Degradation." "Am settled down and hard at work," he wrote to Anna on August 16. "The whole thing, all the conditions of life, the immensity of it, everything is overwhelming. I never conceived such a mass of misery in the world before." The next week he wrote again that his book was one-fifth done: "Am rushing, for I am made sick by this human hellhole called London Town. I find it almost impossible to believe that some of the horrible things I have seen are really so."[19] When he emerged a month later from the jungle, he had the vivid record—manuscript and photographs—ready for the press.

The salient feature of this record is its Blakean compassion. "Of all my books on the long shelf," Jack said near the end of his life, "I love most 'The People of the Abyss.' No other book of mine took so much of my young heart and tears as that study of the economic degradation of the poor" (*Book of Jack London*, I, 381). What affected him most deeply was the hopeless plight of the very old and the inevitable doom of the very young. For example, there are "the Carter" and "the Carpenter," decent, respectable tradesmen who are now too old to compete with vigorous younger men in a ruthless industrial system; their children are dead and with no one to care for them, they have been set loose without shelter or money, to scavenge for bits of garbage along filthy sidewalks and to drift aimlessly and painfully toward death. At the other end of the Abyss are the children; from every one hundred of these, seventy-five will die before the age of five; and perhaps they are the luckier ones—

There is one beautiful sight in the East End, and only one, and it is the children dancing in the street when the organ-grinder goes his round. It is fascinating to watch them, the new-born, the next generation, swaying and stepping, with pretty little mimicries and graceful inventions all their own, with muscles that move swiftly and easily, and bodies that leap airily, weaving rhythms never taught in dancing school. . . . They delight in music, and motion, and color, and very often they betray a startling beauty of face and form under their filth and rags.

But there is a Pied Piper of London Town who steals them away. They disappear. One never sees them again, or anything that suggests them. You may look for them in vain amongst the generation of grown-ups. Here you will find stunted forms, ugly faces, and blunt and stolid minds. Grace, beauty, imagination, all the resiliency of mind and muscle, are gone.[20]

Only the beasts in the jungle remain:

It is rather hard to tell a tithe of what I saw. Much of it is untellable. But in a general way I may say that I saw a nightmare, a fearful slime that quickened the pavement with life, a mess of unmentionable obscenity that put into eclipse the "nightly horror" of Piccadilly and the Strand. . . . They reminded me of gorillas. Their bodies were small, ill-shaped, and squat. There were no swelling muscles, no abundant thews and wide-spreading shoulders. . . . But there was strength in those meagre bodies, the ferocious, primordial strength to clutch and gripe and tear and rend. . . .
But they were not the only beasts that ranged the menagerie. They were only here and there, lurking in dark courts and passing like gray shadows along the walls; but the women from whose rotten loins they spring were everywhere . . . inconceivable types of sodden ugliness, the wrecks of society, the perambulating carcasses, the living deaths—women, blasted by disease and drink till their shame brought not tu'pence in the open mart; and men, in fantastic rags, wrenched by hardship and exposure out of all semblance of men, their faces in a perpetual writhe of pain, grinning idiotically, shambling like apes, dying with every step they took and each breath they drew. . . .
The unfit and the unneeded! . . . The miserable and despised and forgotten, dying in the social shambles. The progeny of prostitution—of the prostitution of men and women and children, of flesh and blood, and sparkle and spirit; in brief, the prostitution of labor. If this is the best that civilization can do for the human, then give us howling and naked savagery. Far better to be a people of the wilderness and desert, of the cave and the squatting-place, than to be a people of the machine and the Abyss. (284–88)

Even with such appalling descriptions of human degradation, *The People of the Abyss* is not merely a sensational diatribe; in the light of the conditions it depicts, the style and tone are remarkably restrained. Jack's compassion was so profound that it overwhelmed his compulsion to preach. He might easily have made the book into a profitable venture in "muckraking"; or, just as easily, he could have made it a useful vehicle for economic propaganda. He deliberately chose to do neither, and he resented the labeling of the work as a "Socialistic treatise": "I merely state the disease as I saw it," he said; "I have not, within the pages of *that* book, stated the cure as I see it" (*Book of Jack London*, I, 381). "*The People of the Abyss* is not a great work," Joan London has written, "but its sincerity places it among the handful of books Jack London wrote because he wanted to, and not merely to make money.... [He] was gratified by the small prestige it brought him among the serious reading public. Some hoped that he would continue to work along the same lines, but the majority of his readers clamored for more fiction. And because his determination to get out of debt and win to financial security had been quickened by his new loathing and fear of poverty, he was glad to accede to their wishes. Later, he would write more about the people of the abyss and kindred subjects."[21]

London's next venture proved to be one of his most profitable works, a novel closely rivaling *The Call of the Wild* and *White Fang* in reprints and total sales, and outranking them in motion picture productions.[22] *The Sea-Wolf* seems to have all the necessary ingredients for greatness. It pulses with the vitality of its creator; it is structured upon the universal, timeless motif of initiation; its setting is likewise archetypal: the ship as microcosm, the eternal sea as most fitting matrix, symbolic as well as literal, for death and rebirth. It also has an excellent cast: convincingly delineated, "round" characters who can stand both as individuals and as representative types—headed by Wolf Larsen, one of the most unforgettable figures in American literature. "It is a rattling good story in one way; something is 'going on' all the time—not always what one would wish, but something. One does not go to sleep over the book," wrote Ambrose Bierce in a letter to George Sterling in 1905. "But the great thing—and it is among the greatest of things—is that tremendous creation, Wolf Larsen. If that is not a permanent addition to literature, it is at least a permanent figure in the memory of the reader. You 'can't lose' Wolf Larsen. He will be with you to the end. So it does not really matter how London has hammered him into you. You may quarrel with the methods, but the result is almost incomparable. The hewing out and setting up of such a figure is enough for a man to do in a life-time. I have hardly words to impart my good judgment of *that* work."[23]

Assuredly it is not easy to "lose" a character who, on the one hand, can quote from memory long passages of Robert Browning's poetry and the Bible and who, on the other, can squeeze a raw potato or a man's arm to a pulp. Praised by Robert Spiller as "London's most fully conceived character" and by Gordon Mills as "London's most enduring example of the intense life,"[24] Larsen is a fascinating composite of Shakespeare's Hamlet, Milton's Satan, Browning's Caliban and Setebos, and Nietzsche's *Übermensch*. But more than this composite, he is the Captain Ahab of literary Naturalism; and he bridges the gap between the Byronic hero and the modern antihero. Like the earlier Romantic hero, Larsen is sensitive, intelligent, domineering, arrogant, uninhibited, actively rebellious against conventional social mores, and—above all—alone. He rules alone; he suffers alone. But, like the twentieth-century man, he lacks purpose and direction. Though he possesses the personal force of Melville's Ahab, he has no quest—not even a mad quest—into which to channel this force; and the result is disorientation, frustration, senseless violence, and finally self-destruction. The thwarting of Larsen's tremendous vitality manifests itself physically in his brutal treatment of his crew and intellectually in his materialistic nihilism:

"Do you know, I am filled with a strange uplift; I feel as if all time were echoing through me, as though all powers were mine. . . . But,"—and his voice changed and the light went out of his face,— "what is this condition in which I find myself? . . . It is what comes when there is nothing wrong with one's digestion, when his stomach is in trim and his appetite has an edge, and all goes well. It is the bribe for living, the champagne of the blood, the effervescence of the ferment—that makes some men think holy thoughts, and other men to see God or to create him when they cannot see him. . . . To-morrow I shall pay for it as the drunkard pays. And I shall know that I must die, at sea most likely, cease crawling of myself to be all acrawl with the corruption of the sea; to be fed upon, to be carrion, to yield up all the strength and movement of my muscles that it may become strength and movement in fin and scale and the guts of fishes.[25]

Physically and morally, Larsen is a prototype of Eugene O'Neill's "Yank" Smith and of T. S. Eliot's ape-neck Sweeney; psychologically, he has more in common with Prufrock and Gerontion—he is cursed with a hyperrational sensibility.[26] In Larsen's gradual deterioration—first headaches, then blindness and paralysis, and finally death from a brain tumor—he is symbolic of a modern type: the psychopathic overreacher who is alienated both from nature and from his fellow man by the leprous disease of self. Jack told his wife Charmian that the underlying motif of *The Sea-Wolf* was that "The superman is anti-social in his tendencies, and in these days of our complex society and sociology he cannot be successful in his hostile aloofness" (*Book of Jack London,* II, 57). Even with his amazing physical strength and his great force of personality, Larsen cannot survive. "It is true that [London] admired, even worshipped, strength," observes Conway Zirkle, "but he had learned that strength was increased by cooperation, by union. The atavistic individual, the lone wolf, was truly a hero, but a tragic hero who was doomed to extinction. The well-integrated group was stronger than any individual could ever be. . . . Those who co-operated won because they were fit. The social virtues, altruism, co-operation—even self-sacrifice—were justified biologically for they made gregarious living possible and the strength of the strong was the strength of the group."[27]

The character best equipped for survival in *The Sea-Wolf* is clearly not Larsen; nor is it the courageous young sailor Johnson, whose survival index is lowered by his readiness to die for the principle of manhood; nor is it the greasy cook, Thomas Mugridge, whose cowardice and meanness fit him for survival only as something less than a man. The character endowed with a potential for survival lacking in these is, curiously enough, a thoroughgoing "sissy" at the beginning of the novel. But the latent adaptability of Humphrey Van Weyden, enhanced by his intelligence, his vital optimism, and his capacity to love, marks him for survival while Larsen is drawn inexorably toward Death, who is his spiritual as well as his literal brother. Van Weyden's rise to self-sustaining maturity and Larsen's decline into paralytic oblivion provide an "X" structure for the novel: Van Weyden starts at the bottom—poles apart from Larsen—and, as he gains in strength and toughness, he moves steadily upward and nearer his demoniacal antagonist. The two lines converge at the moment "Hump" finds the courage to defend Maud Brewster against Larsen's wolfish advances. From this point onward, Larsen's power wanes rapidly. Van Weyden and Miss Brewster escape from the *Ghost* during one of their captor's disabling headache attacks, and the two lines of the "X" begin to diverge. By the time Van Weyden encounters Larsen again, the two are once again, and finally, at opposite extremes: Larsen has lost his crew and is blind and partially paralyzed; Van Weyden has gained a mate and has reached his full maturity.

Van Weyden is the central, if not the most memorable, character in *The Sea-Wolf*; for his growth from effete snobbery into dynamic manhood constitutes the main plot. The sinking of the ferryboat *Martinez*, Van Weyden's immersion, and his dramatic delivery from near-drowning by Larsen signifies the protagonist's rebirth into a raw, unfamiliar world—one of harsh reality where his culture, wealth, and social position are worthless. The first step in his initiation is an awakening to the reality of death as he stares in horror at the alcoholic convulsions of the *Ghost*'s first mate, whose death elicits a volley of oaths from Larsen. "To me," confesses Van Weyden, "death had always been invested with solemnity and dignity. It had been peaceful in its occurrence, sacred in its ceremonial. But death in its more sordid and terrible aspects was a thing with which I had been unacquainted till now" (21).

The next step for Van Weyden is learning the value of hard physical work: "You stand on dead men's legs," Larsen tells him. "You've never had any of your own. You couldn't walk alone between two sunrises and hustle the meat for your belly for three meals. Let me see your hand. . . . Dead men's hands have kept it soft. Good for little else than dish-washing and scullion work" (26). Scorning Van Weyden's demands to be put ashore, Larsen impresses him into the ship's service as a lowly cabin boy —no longer "Mr. Van Weyden" but just plain "Hump"— under the sadistic domination of the Cockney cook; and the ordeal begins during which Van Weyden gradually hardens into manhood. He discovers quickly that the conventions of society, the rules that protect the weak and strong alike, are irrelevant in this new environment: he must survive by countering tooth with claw. He clears his first hurdle in the dramatic knife-sharpening episode with "Cooky": only after he has met the cook's abuse by whetting his own dirk does Hump gain the crew's respect. He is subsequently promoted to first mate and is never again without his knife, the crude metonymy of his manhood.

However, the brutal masculine world of the *Ghost* is no truer than the anemic, utterly feminine world that Van Weyden has left behind. Larsen's bleak materialism is ultimately no better than Van Weyden's blind idealism: the truest philosophy is somewhere between these two extremes in a pragmatic optimism which comprehends the equally real meanness and magnificence of human potentiality. But, to keep man's vision on the stars instead of the slime, the feminine touch is necessary: "It strikes me as unnatural and unhealthful that men should be totally separated from women . . . ," remarks Van Weyden. "Coarseness and savagery are the inevitable results. These men about me should have wives, and sisters, and daughters; then would they be capable of softness, and tenderness, and sympathy. . . . There is no balance in their lives. Their masculinity, which in itself is of the brute, has been overdeveloped. The other and spiritual side of their natures has been dwarfed—atrophied, in fact" (128-29). Neither the emasculating world of social culture nor the brutalizing world of club and fist can produce the truly balanced human being. There must be a sensible equipoise of the two worlds. Until taken aboard the *Ghost*, Van Weyden is only a half-man lacking in virility because he has been reared in a woman's world. Not until he has viewed woman from a man's world is his perspective complete; for only then may he assume his role in society as a full-fledged male—as mate and father.

London's motive for introducing Maud Brewster into the plot of *The Sea-Wolf* was apparently to dramatize Van Weyden's newly-won manhood and fitness for survival. Thematically, the gambit might have been justifiable; but, technically, it was disastrous. From the moment of the incredible coincidence in the middle of the Pacific Ocean when Humphrey Van Weyden, the Dean of American Letters, meets Maud Brewster, the First Lady of American Poetry, *The Sea-Wolf* begins to deteriorate along with Captain Larsen of the *Ghost*. By the time the two lovers have escaped and have become castaways on Endeavor Island, the novel is a sentimental shambles:

> "You are not frightened?" I asked, as I stepped to open the door [of her hut] for her.
> Her eyes looked bravely into mine.
> "And you feel well? perfectly well?"
> "Never better," was her answer.
> We talked a little longer before she went.
> "Good night, Maud," I said.
> "Good night, Humphrey," she said.
> This use of our given names had come about quite as a matter of course, and was as unpremeditated as it was natural. In that moment I could have put my arms around her and drawn her to me. I should certainly have done so out in that world to which we belonged. As it was, the situation stopped there in the only way it could; but I was left alone in my little hut, glowing warmly through and through with a pleasant satisfaction; and I knew that a tie, or a tacit something, existed between us which had not existed before. (296–97)

"The 'love' element, with its absurd suppressions and impossible proprieties, is awful," wrote Ambrose Bierce; "I confess to an overwhelming contempt for both sexless lovers."[28] We find it difficult to demur, even when we realize that a proper Victorian lady and gentleman might have, in fact, behaved just so.[29] London knew exactly what he was doing; he needed another bestseller; and, if pandering to the sentimental popular taste would better his odds, he was willing to gamble his artistic integrity. Yet he was apparently sincere in thinking that the Humphrey-Maud affair was structurally appropriate. In his prospectus of the novel he wrote, "My idea is to take a cultured, refined, super-civilized man and woman (whom the subtleties of artificial, civilized life have blinded to the real facts of life), and throw them into a primitive sea-environment where all is stress and struggle and life expresses itself, simply, in terms of food and shelter; and make this man and woman rise to the situation and come out of it with flying colors." London's intention from the outset was clearly to have a ripping good sea-story with "adventure, storm, struggle, tragedy, and love"; it apparently never entered his mind that the novel might have been made into something greater: "The love-element will run throughout, as the man and woman will occupy the center of the stage pretty much of all the time. Also, it will end happily."[30] The book's immediate success proved that he had written wisely if not too well. What is perhaps most noteworthy is that despite its artistic shortcomings, *The Sea-Wolf* has survived as one of London's most reprinted and most readable novels. Ironically, the villain has saved the hero, as well as the heroine, from a fate worse than death—*i.e.*, from oblivion.

The profitable success of *The Sea-Wolf* enabled London to concern himself with several less mercenary ventures, not the least of which was the intensification of his Socialist activities. In the spiring of 1905 he ran again as the Socialist candidate for the mayoralty of Oakland, receiving almost a thousand votes in defeat (as the Social Labor candidate in 1901 he had received 245 votes). That fall, as the first president of the Intercollegiate Socialist Society, he launched a widely publicized lecture tour which shocked the Establishment and delighted the young radicals. "A great ovation was given Jack London at the Harvard Union," reported Hearst's *Boston American* on Friday, December 22, 1905; "Every available inch of space was occupied; even the gallery was jammed, and the doorways were filled by rows and rows of students. Never before has the student body of Harvard University turned out in such numbers to hear a speaker." Jack obviously told the young people what they wanted to hear. "I went to the University. . . . but I did not find the University alive," he said a few nights later at Yale. "If [collegians] cannot fight for us, we want them to fight against us—of course, sincerely fight against us, believing that the right conduct lies in combating socialism because socialism is a great growing force. But what we do not want is that which obtains today and has obtained in the past of the university, a mere deadness and unconcern and ignorance so far as socialism is concerned. Fight for us or fight against us! Raise your voices one way or the other; be alive!" The student body gave him a standing ovation. "You have mismanaged the world, and it shall be taken from you!" he announced the next week to a meeting of wealthy New Yorkers; "Look at us! We are strong! Consider our hands! They are strong hands, and even now they are reaching forth for all you have, and they will take it, take it by the power of their strong hands; take it from your feeble grasp."[31] This audience did not applaud.

The following spring London started to work on his fiercest literary inoculation, the "first apocalyptic novel of the century," according to Joseph Blotner.[32] "You have failed in your management of society, and your management is to be taken away from you," announces Ernest Everhard, hero of *The Iron Heel*, in his sensational speech to the wealthy Philomaths. "We are going to take your governments, your palaces, and all your purpled ease away from you, and in that day you shall work for your bread even as the peasant in the field or the starved and runty clerk in your metropolises. Here are our hands. They are strong hands!"[33]

The Iron Heel purports to be a copy of the "Everhard Manuscript," a fragment written and hidden away by Avis Everhard, widow of the leader of the "Second [unsuccessful] Revolt," and edited seven centuries later by the historian Anthony Meredith in the year 419 B.O.M. (Brotherhood of Man). Mrs. Everhard's document covers the twenty-year period from 1912-1932 when the capitalist Oligarchy, called "the Iron Heel" by her husband Ernest, rises to complete power, grinding underfoot all opposing political systems. In the early stages of the conflict, Ernest works against this oppression by use of democratic methods, finally winning election to Congress, where he is joined by a half-hundred Socialist representatives.

Realizing the threat to its power, the Plutocracy consolidates its ranks and moves forcefully to suppress all opposition. Union leaders are bought off, secret police and mercenaries are employed as terrorists, and political antagonists are arrested and murdered. Everhard's group is now forced to move underground and to counter violence with violence. The narrative rises to a bloody climax when an oppressed subhuman mob erupts from the great Chicago ghetto and is methodically slaughtered by the mercenaries of the Iron Heel. Although Ernest survives the holocaust and works to reorganize the forces of the Revolution, the manuscript ends abruptly; and we are told in Professor Meredith's concluding footnote that Everhard has been mysteriously executed. Meredith also reminds us that the Oligarchy held its power for another three centuries and throughout numerous Revolts before Herbert Spencer's prophecy of Socialist evolution was at last fulfilled.

Politically speaking, *The Iron Heel* was Jack London's bravest novel. "It was a labor of love, and a dead failure as a book," he later wrote. "The book-buying public would have nothing to do with it, and I got nothing but knocks from the socialists."[34] Though he had not anticipated the hostile Socialist reaction, he did know that the book would be unpopular and that its sales would be limited; nevertheless, he was compelled to write it. The work was motivated by a variety of influences: his experiences in the London slums in 1902 (the climactic chapter of the novel is titled "The People of the Abyss"); the abortive Russian Revolution of 1905; the dramatic events of his own lecture tour that winter; the San Francisco earthquake the following spring, which provided background material for the novel's cataclysmic last chapters; and the reading of W. J. Ghent's *Our Benevolent Feudalism* (1902), which predicted a twentieth-century feudal state dominated by capitalist overlords.[35] London's motivation may also have been sharpened by his unconscious guilt feelings: in 1905, he had used his profits from *The Sea-Wolf* to begin buying land in the Sonoma Valley; and, by the spring of 1906, he was well on his way to creating his own great fief.

Psychologically speaking, *The Iron Heel* is one of Jack's most revealing books; it is the fictional articulation of his private dreams of revolutionary glory. The novel's hero, earnest and "ever-hard," is a fantasy-figure of Jack London purged of his obsession to win to the good life of the American dream. A "natural aristocrat" and a "blond beast" with blacksmith's biceps and prize-fighter's neck, Ernest is Jack's exact physical replica. With his Spencerian *weltanschauung* and his Marxist rhetoric, he is also Jack's metaphysical replica; for, as Joan London remarks, "His best knowledge of the class struggle and the socialist movement, his best speeches and essays he gave to Everhard...." Even the love affair between Ernest and Avis Cunningham Everhard is a replica of that between Jack and Charmian Kittredge London. "Few of Jack London's books, even those which were consciously autobiographical, are so intensely personal," says his daughter.[36] And this personal involvement accounts for the failure of the book as a novel.

There is some merit in Irving Stone's judgment of the book as London's "greatest contribution to the economic revolution," but his claim that it is "one of the most ... beautiful books ever written"[37] is an astonishing lapse of esthetic sensibility. Viewed strictly from the artistic standpoint, *The Iron Heel* is—except for the vivid description of mob violence near the end—a lifeless novel. The hero, haranguing his various audiences with his pretentious ideological pieties, is a relentless boor. The other characters are merely cardboard foils to the much-bruited force of Ernest's magnetic personality and to his irrefutable logic, neither of which is authenticated within the narrative. Time and again we are told of his splendid virtues; seldom are these virtues dramatically discovered through his actions.

And, clearly, a major flaw lies in the telling—in London's unfortunate choice of narrator. Even Professor Meredith's dry, pseudo-scholarly footnotes cannot relieve the cloying sentimentality of Avis Everhard's prose: "When I do not think of what is to come, I think of what has been and is no more—my Eagle, beating with tireless wings the void, soaring toward what was ever his sun, the flaming ideal of human freedom" (2). ". . . Ernest rose before me transfigured, the apostle of truth, with shining brows and the fearlessness of one of God's own angels, battling for the truth and the right, and battling for the succor of the poor and lonely and oppressed. And then there arose before me another figure, the Christ! He, too, had taken the part of the lowly and oppressed, and against all the established power of priest and pharisee. And I remembered his end upon the cross, and my heart contracted with a pang as I thought of Ernest. Was he, too, destined for a cross?—he, with his clarion call and war-noted voice, and all the fine man's vigor of him!" (61). To Avis, Ernest became her "oracle. . . . As I have said, there was never such a lover as he. No girl could live in a university town till she was twenty-four and not have love experiences. I had been made love to by beardless sophomores and gray professors, and by the athletes and the football giants. But not one of them made love to me as Ernest did. . . . Before his earnestness conventional maiden dignity was ridiculous. He

swept me off my feet by the splendid invincible rush of him. . . .
It was unprecedented. It was unreal" (71-72). Moreover, Ernest
"was a humanist and a lover. And he, with his incarnate spirit
of battle, his gladiator body and his eagle spirit—he was as
gentle and tender to me as a poet. He was a poet. A singer in
deeds. And all his life he sang the song of man. And he did it
out of sheer love of man, and for man he gave his life and was
crucified" (182). "And yet he found time in which to love me
and make me happy. But this was accomplished only through
my merging my life completely into his. I learned shorthand
and typewriting, and became his secretary. . . . We loved love,
and our love was never smirched by anything less than the best.
And this out of all remains: I did not fail. I gave him rest—he
who worked so hard for others, my dear, tired-eyed mortalist"
(187). It is *1984* as it might have been penned by Elizabeth
Barrett Browning.

But, if it is less than an artistic success, *The Iron Heel* must
nevertheless be regarded as an important book. It was enthusiastically commended by Eugene V. Debs, Leon Trotsky, and
Anatole France. Robert E. Spiller has called it "a terrifying forecast of Fascism and its evils"; Philip Foner ventures that it is
"probably the most amazingly prophetic work of the twentieth
century"; Maxwell Geismar suggests that it is "a key work—
perhaps a classic work—of American radicalism"; Walter B.
Rideout classifies it as "a minor revolutionary classic"; and Max
Lerner concludes that "The real point about *The Iron Heel* is
not what Jack London failed to foresee, but how remarkably
much he did foresee."[38] What he failed mainly to foresee was
that the middle class would not only survive but actually grow
stronger through the capitalistic system. But what he did foresee was man's inexhaustible capacity for oppression and violence even in the midst of economic prosperity. And his apocalyptic vision of urban holocaust still has a disquieting immediacy.

The Iron Heel is also significant for another reason. It represents one of London's major fictional modes: fantasy. Much of
his writing in this genre is "transitive," that is, it is intended to
serve some purpose more important in the author's mind than
mere art or entertainment. Such is the obvious case with *The Iron
Heel,* which is little more than an ideological treatise cast in

narrative form, as are shorter fictions like "The Dream of Debs," a vision of the triumph of organized labor by means of a great General Strike; "The Strength of the Strong," a parable which dramatizes the superiority of collective strength over individual power; "The Minions of Midas," an early potboiler about a group of homicidal blackmailers who label themselves as the inevitable "culmination of industrial and social wrong [,] the successful failures of the age, the scourges of a degraded civilization"; and "Goliah," the juvenile tale of a mild-mannered little scientist who invents a machine to stop all wars and who is subsequently loved by all mankind "for his simplicity and comradeship and warm humanness, and for his fondness for salted pecans and his aversion to cats." However, Jack's appetence for fantasy may be traced to something subtler and deeper than his desire to propagandize.

III   *Fearful Fantasies*

Deep down in the roots of the race is fear. It came first into the world, and it was the dominant emotion in the primitive world. To-day, for that matter, it remains the most firmly seated of the emotions.   —Jack London, "The Terrible and Tragic in Fiction"

Startling as it may be to think of Jack London and Edgar Allan Poe as literary bedfellows, their careers, minds, and personalities were comparable in several ways. Both were masters of the art of the short story. Both were also moody, often lonely individuals who yearned for the securities of home, companionship, and love —and whose basic insecurities were concealed under the cloak of reckless egotism only to be manifest in a weakness for alcohol and in a genius for oneiric fiction. Thanks to Princess Marie Bonaparte, Gaston Bachelard, and other French analysts, Poe's dark secrets have long since become part of the public domain. London's critical psychoanalysis, on the other hand, has barely begun, although Maxwell Geismar made a start in *Rebels and Ancestors* when he observed that it is the "world of dream and fantasy and desolate, abnormal emotion that [London] inhabits far more completely than the world of people and society—for all his stress on that" (186).[39]

London's fantasies may not constitute his best work, but they are both readable and revealing. As with Poe, they disclose more about the author than he probably realized; and they are often not an escape from reality so much as a symbolic path into the deeper, inchoate reality of the unconscious mind. Seldom overt, ·the clues to the telltale heart of this dark world are the images and metaphors which set the story's mood. Almost without exception London's fantasies are woven within a framework of violence and death; they are textured by metaphors of darkness, chaos, pain, and terror; seldom do they end happily. Their characteristic attitude is one of fear and trembling. In one novel only (*The Star Rover*) do we find a concluding affirmation, and it is for the next world, not this one. Apocalyptic gloom over-shadows the rest. "Putting the horror-story outside the pale, can any story be really great, the theme of which is anything but tragic and terrible?" London asked rhetorically. "It would not seem so. The great stories in the world's literary treasure-house seem all to depend upon the tragic and terrible for their strength and greatness" (*Jack London Reports*, 334).

The dear old sacred terror intrigued Jack as it intrigued Henry James:

> What is it that lures boys to haunted houses after dark, compelling them to fling rocks and run away with their hearts going so thun-derously pit-a-pat as to drown the clatter of their flying feet? What is it that grips a child, forcing it to listen to ghost stories which drive it into ecstasies of fear, and yet forces it to beg for more and more? . . . Is it a stirring of the savage in them?—of the savage who has slept, but never died, since the time the river-folk crouched over the fires of their squatting-places, or the tree-folk bunched to-gether and chattered in the dark?   (*Jack London Reports*, 331–32)

This same phenomenon is central to London's most popular "dream vision": *Before Adam*, written in forty days, completed on June 7, 1906, and published that fall in *Everybody's Magazine* (*Letters from Jack London*, 327). Jack attested that he wrote the book to show "(1) the mistakes and lost off-shoots in the process of biologic evolution; and (2) that in a single generation the only device primitive man, in my story, invented, was the carry-ing of water and berries in gourds" (*Letters from Jack London*, 332); but neither of these things speaks to the continuing appeal of the story or to its true significance, which is psychological and mythic. "Pictures! Pictures! Pictures!" begins the narrative. "Often, before I learned, did I wonder whence came the multitudes of pictures that thronged my dreams; for they were pictures the like of which I had never seen in real wake-a-day life. They tormented my childhood, making of my dreams a procession of nightmares and a little later convincing me that I was different from my kind, a creature unnatural and accursed."[40]

The narrator of *Before Adam* has a recurrent dream which takes him back to a previous existence as one of man's remote ancestors in the mid-Pleistocene Age. He dreams his life as Big Tooth, who is one of the Folk caught between monkey-like Tree People and the advanced Fire People (*homo sapiens*), and who is threatened not only by these but also by the terrifying presence of "Red-Eye, the atavism," within the Folk tribe: "Ogres and bugaboos and I had been happy bed-fellows, compared with these terrors that made their bed with me throughout my childhood, and still bed with me, now, as I write this, full of years" (11).

Yet, filled as Big Tooth's life is with misery and danger, it is not devoid of happiness. There is "the peace of the cool caves in the cliffs, the circus of the drinking-places at the end of the day. . . . the bite of the morning wind in the tree-tops, [and] the taste of young bark sweet in your mouth" (2-3). There is also the companionship of his bosom friend Lop-Ear, steadfast, affectionate, protective—who possesses, in short, the traits normally associated with a good parent. For instance, Lop-Ear risks his own life to save Big-Tooth from the arrows of the deadly Fire-Men:

I often meditate upon this scene—the two of us, half-grown cubs, in the childhood of the race, and the one mastering his fear, beating down his selfish impulse of flight, in order to stand by and succor the other. And there rises up before me all that was there foreshadowed, and I see visions of Damon and Pythias, of life-saving crews and Red Cross nurses, of martyrs and leaders of forlorn hopes, of Father Damien, and of the Christ himself, and of all the men of earth, mighty of stature, whose strength may trace back to the elemental loins of Lop-Ear and Big-Tooth and other dim denizens of the Younger World. (91–92)

And, above all, Big-Tooth has the precarious happiness of freedom—freedom from the restrictions of social conformity, freedom for adventure and exploration.

In an episode rich with Freudian implications, Big-Tooth defies the brutal authority of Red-Eye and has to run away for safety along with Lop-Ear. Forced out of the security of their small cave by Red-Eye, set to flight by this avenging father-figure, deprived of the protection of a natural as well as symbolic mother, the two youths begin their long journey into the vast unknown: "a desolate land of rocks and foaming streams and clattering cataracts. . . . mighty canyons and gorges . . . [and] in all directions, range upon range, the unceasing mountains. . . . And then, at last, one hot midday, dizzy with hunger, we gained the divide. From this high backbone of earth, to the north, across the diminishing down-falling ranges, we caught a glimpse of a far lake. The sun shone upon it, and about it were open, level grasslands, while to the eastward we saw the dark line of a wide-stretching forest" (155-56).

From the lofty reaches of the world spine, the young hero and his companion descend to the world center, a region of incredible abundance where the streams are "packed thick with salmon that had come up from the sea to spawn" and are surrounded by rich grasslands. Moving eastward from this matrix of fecundity, "We came out upon the river, but we did not know it for our river. We had been lost so long that we had come to accept the condition of being lost as habitual. As I look back I see clearly how our lives and destinies are shaped by the merest chance. We did not know it was our river—there was no way of telling; and if we had never crossed it we would most probably have never returned to the horde; and I, the modern, the thousand centuries yet to be born, would never have been born" (157).

Because of "merest chance," however, Big-Tooth achieves his rebirth, finally returns to his tribe, mates with the Swift One, and becomes the father of many children, thus maintaining the long line of descent between his primal world and the civilized one of the narrator. In mythological terms, Big-Tooth's story is a re-creation of the "rites of passage" archetype; it is more-over, a fictive manifestation of what Mircea Eliade has called "the myth of the eternal return"—man's universal compulsion to return to the beginning of things and to the innocence and simplicity of the childhood of the race. But London does not conclude the novel on this happy note; instead, the countenance of the terrible Red-Eye leaves a last, haunting impression on the narrator's memory: "I can see him now, as I write this, scowling, his eyes inflamed, as he peers about him at the circle of the Tree People. And he crooks one monstrous leg and with his gnarly toes scratches himself on the stomach. He is Red-Eye, the atavism." So the vision, originated in fear, ends on the characteristic note of ominous terror.

The same vision, along with its atavistic theme, reappears in *The Scarlet Plague,* published in 1912. In this work London demonstrates that Red-Eye, the archetypal monster of the id, has never been eradicated from the racial unconscious; he has only been slumbering within us, awaiting the right moment to leap forward in all his terrifying brutality. In *The Scarlet Plague,* London provides that moment in the form of a cataclysmic epidemic which sweeps over the world, wiping out most of its inhabitants. The germ of this story may be discovered in Poe's "The Masque of the Red Death," wherein the symptoms are described as "sharp pains, and sudden dizziness, and then dissolution [,] the whole seizure, progress, and termination [being] the incidents of half an hour." The symptoms of the scarlet plague are similar: "Many died within ten or fifteen minutes of the appearance of the first signs. . . . Usually, they had convulsions at the time of the appearance of the [scarlet] rash. . . . And another strange thing was the rapidity of decomposition. No sooner was a person dead than the body seemed . . . to melt away even as you looked at it. That was one of the reasons the plague spread so rapidly. All the billions of germs in a corpse were so immediately released."[41]

In addition to the disease, Jack also borrowed the theme of Poe's story: the idea that no man can escape the terrible realities of disease and death—or that all men ultimately share the brotherhood of mortality. Just as Poe's Prince Prospero and his followers try to shut out the contagious sufferings of their fellow men, so London's hero and his colleagues at the University of California blockade themselves in the massive Chemistry Building. And just as surely as the Red Death follows Prospero's vainglorious court through the sealed portals of the castellated abbey, so the scarlet plague filters through the barricaded walls of Science's ivory tower. Only James Howard Smith—not a scientist, but a professor of English—escapes to witness civilization disintegrating in chaos and red terror.

From the point of his hero's escape, London departs from Poe's tale. The long-journey motif manifests itself as Smith wanders through the desolated land in search of some remnant of humanity. For three years, almost crazy from loneliness, he searches for some fellow human being who has survived the devastation of the plague. Finally, in the region of Lake Temescal, California, he finds the signs of humanity—but, instead of an intelligent, sensitive, refined creature of his own kind, he stumbles across the thing that his race is to become: the atavism, "a large, dark hairy man, heavy-jawed, slant-browed, fierce-eyed." In this book he is called "the Chauffeur," but his brutish characteristics are the same as those of Red-Eye in *Before Adam,* and the force symbolized in him has survived the plague to carry mankind back to the primeval wilderness.

The narrator observes a vicious irony in the survival of this "iniquitous moral monster" while millions of better men died—but he also notes a grim poetic justice. By the time of the plague, 2013 A.D., the United States had developed into a totalitarian plutocracy, the mass of its population in bondage to the wealthy, physically degenerate upper classes. Without realizing it, men of intellectual and esthetic refinement had sown the seeds of destruction within the very lap of their society: "In the midst of our civilization, down in our slums and laborghettos, we had bred a race of barbarians, of savages; and now, in the time of our calamity, they turned upon us like the wild beasts they were and destroyed us" (105-6).

After the plague, the Chauffeur had discovered another survivor, Vesta Van Warden, beautiful young widow of one of the world's richest men ("Warden" of wealth and keeper of the keys for an oppressive economic system). Though she fled in terror, she was finally caught, beaten, subdued, and mated to this coarse epitome of lower-class brutality, who gloats over his new social position:

"We've got to start all over and replenish the earth and multiply. You're handicapped, Professor. You ain't got no wife, and we're up against a regular Garden-of-Eden proposition. But I ain't proud. I'll tell you what, Professor." He pointed at their little infant, barely a year old. "There's your wife, though you'll have to wait till she grows up. It's rich, ain't it. We're all equals here, and I'm the biggest toad in the splash." (158–59)

But the Chauffeur is not Ernest Everhard in loin cloth, and *The Scarlet Plague* is not a primitivistic re-run of *The Iron Heel*. Allowing mood to overshadow message, London creates a much more telling indictment of twentieth-century civilization than in his idea-ridden earlier novel. As occasionally happened in his fantasies, the compulsion to preach is forgotten in the heat of the poetic moment. The English professor who watched his world vanish in a "sheet of flame and a breath of death" is now an old man known as "Granser" who, standing at the end of time, is trying bravely to shore up the ruins of a once-mighty civilization:

" 'The fleeting systems lapse like foam,' " he mumbled what was evidently a quotation. "That's it—foam and fleeting. All man's toil upon the planet was just so much foam. He domesticated the serviceable animals, destroyed the hostile ones, and cleared the land of its wild vegetation. And then he passed, and the flood of primordial life rolled back again, sweeping his handiwork away—the weeds and the forest inundated the fields, the beasts of prey swept over his flocks, and now there are wolves on the Cliff House beach." He was appalled by the thought. "Where four million people disported themselves, the wild wolves roam to-day, and the savage progeny of our loins, with prehistoric weapons, defend themselves against the fanged despoilers." (33–34)

Apocalyptic pessimism notwithstanding, the conclusion of *The Scarlet Plague* has a wild, lyrical beauty reminiscent of the final note of mythic rapture in *The Call of the Wild*. Often in London's work, when his outlook for man in civilization is bleakest, his vision of nature's eternal fecundity—his mystical faith in the strength of the life force itself—presents itself most powerfully. The ebbing of his faith in social reform seems to have been accompanied by a tendency to turn more and more for solace toward the seemingly inexhaustible vitality of nature. The dramatic power of his conclusion to *The Scarlet Plague* derives from the tension between these two forces: a civilization tottering on its last leg (symbolized in the figure of the old man who has narrated the story) and the animation of nature in her wilder forms (signified in the concluding tableau of the horses, mountain lions, sea lions, and skin-clad boy):

Edwin was looking at a small herd of wild horses which had come down on the hard sand. There were at least twenty of them, young colts and yearlings and mares, led by a beautiful stallion which stood in the foam at the edge of the surf, with arched neck and bright wild eyes, sniffing the salt air from off the sea.

"What is it?" Granser queried.

"Horses," was the answer. "First time I ever seen 'em on the beach. It's the mountain lions getting thicker and thicker and driving 'em down."

The low sun shot red shafts of light, fan-shaped, up from a cloud-tumbled horizon. And close at hand, in the white waste of shore-lashed waters, the sea-lions, bellowing their old primeval chant, hauled up out of the sea on the black rocks and fought and loved.

"Come on, Granser," Edwin prompted.

And the old man and boy, skin-clad and barbaric, turned and went along the right of way into the forest in the wake of the goats. (180–81)

This final vivid montage is as fine as anything London ever created. For a moment, sea and wilderness are fused in the image of the stallion that stands triumphantly at the water's edge. The foam image, used earlier to symbolize the fleeting systems of man, now assumes an additional dimension—that of the eternal fecundity of the sea, that mighty womb from which life emerges and to which life returns in a never-ending cycle. Against a backdrop of crimson sky, white waters, and black rocks, the timeless pageant of fighting and loving—of life itself—is enacted by the sea lions. And, lurking always in the background, is the grim specter of Darwinistic survival, nature red in tooth and claw, suggested in the image of the mountain lions. Juxtaposed against these primal natural forces is the bent, pathetic figure of the old man, the last remnant of a dying culture.

More complex both thematically and structurally than either *Before Adam* or *The Scarlet Plague* is *The Star Rover*, published the year before London's death. This strange novel, ignored by most of London's critics, is perhaps the most difficult of all his works to assess fairly. Maxwell Geismar dismisses it as "incredibly bad"; Irving Stone calls it "a magnificent literary accomplishment."[42] Joan London has made the most cogent assessment: "Into this extraordinary and little-known book he flung with a prodigal hand riches which he had hoarded for years, and compressed into brilliant episodes notes originally intended for full-length books. Of all his later work, only portions of this novel and a few short stories reveal the fulfillment of the artistic promise so evident in his early writing" (*Jack London and His Times*, 362). Even in praising the novel Miss London indicates the source of its principal weakness, which is structural: where London should have concentrated on one narrative, he tried to handle a half-dozen, thus vitiating the effect of his central theme.

The main plot of the novel is based on the experiences of an ex-convict named Ed. Morrell, who appears as one of the characters. Morrell's own story, published as *The Twenty-Fifth Man* in 1924, is as fantastic as London's fictional account in *The Star Rover*. One of a band of rancher-outlaws who fought the railroad monopoly, the "octopus" indicted in Frank Norris's famous novel, Morrell was convicted and sentenced to a life-term in the California prisons. During his several years of imprisonment he endured incredible tortures. One of the most diabolical devices for punishing intractable inmates was "the jacket," a heavy canvas square into which the prisoner was tightly laced for several days until his spirit was broken. After almost dying in the jacket, Morrell mastered a form of self-hypnosis (astral projection) which, he claimed, enabled him to leave his physical body and travel at will through both time and space. After receiving a pardon by the governor of California in 1909 (an event that Morrell had predicted four years earlier), he devoted his life to penal reform. He met Jack London in 1912, and he gives the following brief account of their relationship:

Jack London and I were very dear friends, and we had often talked about my experiences in the dungeon, particularly those phases pertaining to the "little death" in the strait-jacket. . . .

"God, Ed., do you know what this means to me?" he often said. "It has been the ambition of my life to put across a staggering punch against the whole damnable, rotten American Jail System. I want it to be my masterpiece."[43]

If *The Star Rover* is not "the staggering punch" that London wanted, it is not a dull book. Taking Morrell's story as the basis for his main narrative, London added a series of soul-flight adventures, any one of which would have made a marketable short story: Darrell Standing, the narrator, though astral projection relives parts of former lives as (1) the French Count Guillaume Sainte-Marie, who loves and fences during the late Renaissance in the best Dumas style; (2) the youth Jesse Fancher, who, traveling with a wagon train from Arkansas, is killed by the Mormons and Indians in the notorious Mountain Meadow Massacre; (3) a fourth-century Christian ascetic who inhabits a tiny cave in the Egyptian desert; (4) Adam Strang, a blond superman who fights nobly against the "yellow peril" in the sixteenth-century Orient; (5) the herculean Dane, Ragnar Lodbrog, who is captured in a battle with the Roman Army and subsequently becomes a legionary officer under Pilate during the time of the Crucifixion; (6) Daniel Foss, a castaway who lives for eight years on a desert island during the early nineteenth century. In addition to these major projections, other fragmentary reincarnations take Darrell Standing back to prehistoric existences.

But *The Star Rover* is considerably more than a loose-knit sequence of adventure stories. A cogent exposé of a corrupt, brutalizing penal system, it "truly states prison conditions," as London wrote to Roland Phillips, editor of *Cosmopolitan*: "It is the law to-day that a man can be hanged by the neck until dead, for punching another man in the nose. . . . It is also legal in California to sentence a man to life-imprisonment in solitary. . . . I have really understated the severity of the use of the jacket" (*Letters from Jack London*, 418). However, more than an exposé, it may be compared as a dramatic tribute to man's historic capacity for suffering with such novels as Arthur

Koestler's *Darkness at Noon* and Bernard Malamud's *The Fixer.*

But most intriguing of all is London's philosophical ground-shifting. Gone are his hard-nosed materialism and scientific rationalism; instead, we encounter a curious mixture of idealism, mysticism, and metempsychosis. "The key-note of the book is: THE SPIRIT TRIUMPHANT," wrote London (*Letters from Jack London,* 419). He contended that he was deliberately playing tricks with philosophy in order to appeal to the widest possible audience, but more probably—and more characteristically—he was playing tricks on himself in refusing to acknowledge the nonrational element that was a vital part of his creative genius—a natural gift inherited from his spiritualist mother. "We know life only phenomenally, as a savage may know a dynamo," Darrell Standing muses; "but we know nothing of life noumenonally, nothing of the nature of the intrinsic stuff of life. . . . I say, and as you, my reader, realize, I speak with authority—I say that matter is the only illusion."[44] Wolf Larsen had asserted with equal authority that "life is a mess . . . a thing that moves and may move for a minute, an hour, a year, or a hundred years, but that in the end will cease to move"; but this Naturalistic view was small comfort to a writer whose own once-magnificent physique had begun to deteriorate from too many years of too little exercise and too much drink, too much work and too little rest. "I have lived millions of years. I have possessed many bodies, . . ." exclaims Darrell Standing; "I am life. I am the unquenched spark ever flashing and astonishing the face of time, ever working my will and wreaking my passion on the cloddy aggregates of matter, called bodies, which I have transiently inhabited" (123). Perhaps death and dissolution were not the words final, after all—"For look you. This finger of mine, so quick with sensation, so subtle to feel, so delicate in its multifarious dexterities, so firm and strong to crook and bend or stiffen by means of cunning leverages—this finger is not I. Cut it off. I live. The body is mutilated. I am not mutilated. The spirit that is I, is whole" (123).

Soul flight! This might indeed be an escape from the old biological trap, a release of the triumphant spirit from its decaying prison-house. Unfortunately, escape from the old American trap—Success—was another matter.

IV *Another American Tragedy*

Martin Eden lived only for himself, fought only for himself, and, if you please, died for himself. He fought for entrance into the bourgeois circles where he expected to find refinement, culture, high-living and high-thinking. He won his way into those circles and was appalled by the colossal, unlovely mediocrity of the bourgeoisie. He fought for a woman he loved and had idealized. He found that love had tricked him and failed him, and that he had loved his idealization more than the woman herself. These were the things he had found life worth living in order to fight for. When they failed him, being a consistent Individualist, being unaware of the collective human need, there remained nothing for which to live and fight. And so he died.

　　　　　—Jack London, letter to the Rev. Charles Brown (1910)

　　The following comment was written not by a college student, nor by a literary critic, but by a well-educated, successful young businessman. It is cited not merely because it is an honest, unsolicited testimonial but because it so accurately reflects a common response to what is considered London's most intensely personal novel: "... I have for the past two evenings been absorbed completely (and I do mean *completely*) in *Martin Eden*. I am profoundly moved. Nothing else I have ever read has had this effect upon me and I am not capable of analyzing it just yet."[45]
　　Although its artistic merits may be open to question, *Martin Eden* is a profoundly moving book for many readers; and any serious attempt to assess Jack London's work must involve this novel. Critics—those who have taken the trouble to read it—have variously considered it to be his best book or his worst book. Franklin Walker is probably closest to the mark in saying it is one of London's most puzzling books, for although it is "uneven in structure, sometimes clumsy in expression, at times mawkish in tone [,] it possesses great lasting power, having more vitality today than it did the day it issued from the press."[46] *Martin Eden* has maintained its power for several reasons: it belongs to a fictional genre which never seems to lose its appeal for sensitive, youthful readers; it is archetypal both in theme and in structure; it articulates an especially potent cultural myth; and it is tremendously charged with London's personal vitality.
　　Martin Eden is part of a literary tradition which includes such

classics as Goethe's *Wilhelm Meister's Apprenticeship*, Melville's *Pierre*, Somerset Maugham's *Of Human Bondage*, D. H. Lawrence's *Sons and Lovers*, and Thomas Wolfe's *Look Homeward, Angel*. A *bildungsroman* or "education novel," its basic pattern involves the hero's painful transition from a state of innocence into one of "knowing"; and, because *Martin Eden* is drawn largely from London's own formative ordeal as a writer, it is necessarily an agonized—and agonizing—novel.

In the plot, which is relatively straightforward and uncomplicated, a husky sailor rescues a young gentleman from the attack of a gang of waterfront toughs and is rewarded by an invitation to the luxurious home of the stranger, Arthur Morse. The sailor is, significantly, twenty-one years old when he is introduced into this dazzling new world of upper, middle-class refinement. Lacking in manners and formal education, he is nevertheless sensitive and intelligent. He meets and immediately falls in love with Arthur's pale, ethereally beautiful sister Ruth, who—university educated, exquisitely poised, articulate—is wholly unlike any girl he has ever met. Inspired to become worthy of this genteel goddess, Martin Eden becomes ambitious: he quits drinking, smoking, and swearing, starts bathing and brushing his teeth regularly, presses his trousers, and initiates a rigorous program of self-education through the local lending-library. Though Ruth does not at first share his powerful infatuation, she is amused by his valiant efforts at self-improvement and fascinated by his immense vitality; she volunteers to become his cultural tutor, and they begin to see each other regularly.

Martin learns with amazing rapidity and within a few months has become conversant not only with the best-known writers but also with philosophers like Adam Smith, Karl Marx, Henry George, and, above all, Herbert Spencer; but, the more he learns, the more clearly he sees the hollowness and hypocrisy of the Morse world. Ruth's parents become alarmed about Martin's radicalism and about the possibility that their daughter is becoming attached to this wild young man. When Ruth finds herself falling in love with him and urges him to find a steady, respectable occupation, Martin decides to embark upon a career in writing. He rents a typewriter, sets himself to work in a frenzy of creativity, allows himself no more than five hours of sleep a

night, and grinds out stories, articles, poems, and jokes by the
dozen. Then after pawning his bicycle, his only decent suit,
and his overcoat to buy stamps, he waits for word from the
magazine editors: that word is *No* as manuscript after manuscript comes back.

Broke and desperate, Martin takes a job in the laundry at
a large resort hotel where he becomes a fourteen-hour-day
work-beast. After several weeks of this drudgery, he quits and
returns again to the frustrating cycle of rejected manuscripts.
Only Russ Brissenden, a brilliant but cynical poet, assures him
that his work shows genuine talent—too genuine for the cheap
commercialized literary marketplace. All the others—friends,
relatives, Ruth—keep nagging him to get a steady job; and,
when Martin is falsely publicized in the local newspapers as a
notorious revolutionary, Ruth rejects him. Shortly afterwards,
he learns that his closest companion Brissenden has committed
suicide. Exhausted by his ordeal and profoundly depressed by
these personal tragedies, Martin lapses into a neurasthenic daze.
Almost simultaneously he starts to receive acceptances for the
many manuscripts he has sent out; his success snowballs; he is
lionized by the cultural élite; the magazines and publishers
clamor for his stuff; and Ruth comes back, begging his forgive-
ness and declaring her love. But she is too late. Disenchanted
and passive, he books passage on a ship to the South Seas. Halfway across the Pacific Ocean, he squeezes through a porthole,
drops into the ocean, and at last finds peace.

Discernible even in this rough summary is the larger structural
pattern of the novel: the hero emerges from the sea at the outset
and returns to the sea at the end. The ocean metaphor, usually
set forth in nautical imagery, recurs throughout and serves to
unify the novel. When Martin first enters the Morse home, he
feels as if he were on the unsteady deck of a ship in rough seas;
and one of the first sights his eyes focus on is an oil painting
of a pilot-schooner surging through a heavy sea against a stormy
sunset sky; later in the evening, he likens himself to "a sailor,
in a strange ship, on a dark night, groping about in the unfamiliar
running rigging" (10). These images are prophetic as well as
descriptive: during his nervous breakdown, he thinks of him-

self as "chartless and rudderless" with no port to make, as drifting nowhere (349).

Set against the sea and providing the basic tension of the novel is the metaphor of the trap. Martin feels he is being led into a cage like some wild animal on display when he enters the Morse house, which, though spacious by society's standards, is a dark, cramped cell by natural standards—by the perspectives of the ocean which have hitherto set the reaches of Martin's vision: "The wide rooms seemed too narrow for his rolling gait, and to himself he was in terror lest his broad shoulders should collide with the doorways or sweep the bric-a-brac from the low mantel" (1). And, though his intellectual horizons are widened, the image of the trap recurs with increasing force as the novel progresses. From the sea, Martin's Garden of Eden, he has moved first into the stuffy hothouse of Victorian gentility represented by the Morses; from that, into the stifling hell of the steam laundry, where he suffers through a midsummer's nightmare of killing toil; and then to the living tomb at Maria Silva's house, where he sleeps, studies, writes, and keeps house in a cubicle so small that two-thirds of the total space is used up by his bed. In brief, his quest for knowledge, imaged at first in the cold, white light of the stars, has led him down a progressively narrowing blind tunnel to the tiny cabin aboard the steamship *Mariposa* (Spanish for "night taper").[47]

Like all education novels, *Martin Eden* is a book about *seeing*. Early in the story we are told that our young hero "saw with wide eyes, and he could tell what he saw. . . . He communicated his power of vision, till they saw with his eyes what he had seen" (20). But, though this power of vision is the key to his artistic genius, Martin is blinded by his false romantic idol: he does not see Ruth at all when he enters the Morse home; he sees a lovely, golden-haloed princess. "No, she was a spirit, a divinity, a goddess; such sublimated beauty was not of the earth. Or perhaps the books were right, and there were many such as she in the upper walks of life. She might well be sung by that chap Swinburne" (4–5). Ruth, whose very name is a mockery, is a lifeless spirit; and she might truly have been celebrated by Algernon Swinburne, the notorious versifier of *fin-de-siècle* Victorianism; therefore, it is fitting that Martin finds himself recalling Swinburne in his cabin aboard the *Mariposa*. It is also fitting that his state of apathy which precedes this last voyage is represented by a corresponding vagueness in the images of his reveries: "Once in his rooms, he dropped into a Morris chair and sat staring straight before him.... Then his mind went blank again, and the pictures began to form and vanish under his eyelids. There was nothing distinctive about the pictures. They were always masses of leaves and shrub-like branches shot through with hot sunshine.... It was not restful, that green foliage. The sunlight was too raw and glaring. It hurt him to look at it, and yet he looked, he knew not why" (388, 396). In other words, Martin has lost his sense of focus, and his sight is without insight.

Martin Eden is a story about the Dark Fall—about the price man has been condemned to pay for the unhappy gift of knowledge. Martin, as *sea*-man, is happy, innocent, unselfconscious, naturally graceful: Adam before the Fall. Ruth, his Eve, acts as his guide to the deadly fruit of knowledge. As he emerges from the Edenic sea and enters her world, he becomes for the first time in his life *self*-conscious, shamed by his social and intellectual nakedness: "All his life, up to then, he had been unaware of being either graceful or awkward. Such thoughts of self had never entered his mind.... He felt lost, alone there in the room with that pale spirit of a woman" (6). It is a premonition of his ultimate disaster, his lostness and aloneness.

Viewed symbolically, Martin's "education" is a growth in consciousness: a breaking away from the primal rhythms of the unconscious—symbolized by the sea—into the fractured world of over-reason—culture, intellect, civilization. As Lizzie Connolly tells him, his sickness is in his "think machine." Martin's is also the universal sickness of modern man caught in the Naturalistic trap—the same "middle stage" Theodore Dreiser defined so poignantly at the beginning of Chapter 17 in *Sister Carrie*: "... scarcely beast, in that [he] is no longer wholly guided by instinct; scarcely human, in that [he] is not yet wholly guided by reason.... As a beast, the forces of life aligned him with them; as a man, he has not yet wholly learned to align himself with the forces. In this intermediate stage he wavers—neither drawn in harmony with nature by his instincts nor yet wisely putting himself into harmony by his own free will."

Unable to regain his former state, intolerably miserable in his present state, Martin falls inevitably into the pattern of eternal return. Carl Jung, echoing Herman Melville's Ishmael, has written that "the way of the soul in search of its lost father—like Sophia seeking Bythos—leads to the water, to the dark mirror that reposes at its bottom. . . . This water is no figure of speech, but a living symbol of the dark psyche." Or, as he observes elsewhere, "The sea is the favourite symbol for the unconscious, the mother of all that lives."[48] Jung's remarks provide the clue to the last lines of *Martin Eden*: "And somewhere at the bottom he fell into darkness. That much he knew. He had fallen into darkness. And at the instant he knew, he ceased to know" (411). The resolution of the novel's underlying tension—the paradox of knowing and unknowing, sight and insight, light and darkness—is as fine as any ending London ever wrote; and though many critics have objected that the reader is not properly prepared for Martin's death, London's closure is artistically superb.

Martin Eden, in addition to its universal appeal, has special impact upon the American reader because it involves one of the most potent myths in the American culture, the Dream of Rags-to-Riches, and because its hero so clearly represents the values of that culture even while ostensibly rejecting them. London had originally selected the title "Success" for his novel, with "Star-Dust" his second choice.[49] Either would have been appropriate, but neither would have been quite so fitting as the name of the hero himself;[50] for "Martin Eden" is a symbolic epitome of the archetypal American male: "Martin," the "man of war," incongruously gifted with the innocence of "Eden," deadly but incorruptible; the American Adam who, despite his pure white soul, is as D. H. Lawrence tells us, "a man with a gun." Martin Eden belongs to that long, red line of Adamic warriors in American literature headed by Leatherstocking and followed by such characters as Henry Fleming, Frederick Henry, Francis Macomber, and Ike McCaslin.

But Martin is also a member of another American literary fraternity comprising Horatio Alger, Frank Algernon Cowper-

wood, and Jay Gatsby. Like Gatsby especially, Martin is destroyed ultimately by the delusions that an ideal goal may be
attained through material means and that success is synony-
mous with happiness. He also shares with Gatsby the vague confusion of the Dream with the decadent avatar of Courtly-Love
mythology—the notion that the true knight may achieve blessed-
ness simply by winning the princess. Martin's inability to see
that the girl of his dreams, like the world of which she is a
representative product, is not golden but merely gilded is—in
the same way as Gatsby's—symptomatic of his greater blindness
in his quest. Gatsby's Daisy, we finally learn, is nothing but a
voice full of money; Martin's Ruth, a silver laugh—"like tinkling
silver bells" (9). Both are cold, hollow women, and both have
a false ring. But in their culture it is not the substance but the
image that counts. Gatsby and Martin fail to understand this,
just as they fail to realize that in America the value is in the
process, not in the product. *Work performed* is the phrase that
haunts Martin's brain:

> "It was work performed! And now you feed me, when then you
> let me starve, forbade me your house, and damned me because I
> wouldn't get a job. And the work was already done, all done. And
> now, when I speak, you check the thought unuttered on your lips
> and hang on my lips and pay respectful attention to whatever I
> choose to say. . . . And why? Because I'm famous; because I've a lot
> of money. Not because I'm Martin Eden. . . ." (378)

The important thing is the appearance, not the essence; the
joy is in becoming, not in being. And that is why, having arrived,
Martin, like Gatsby, finds himself nowhere, and why, therefore,
he has nothing left except to die.

Martin Eden can not be trusted as Jack London's spiritual
autobiography—unlike Martin, Jack was fully aware of "the
collective human need" and lived for much more than himself—
yet the novel still has a certain symbolic credibility and an
element of prophecy. Youthful vitality is the key to Martin
Eden's charismatic appeal, and the profligate expenditure of
this tremendous energy is the key to his tragedy—just as it is
the key to London's own personal tragedy. London was no

suicide,[51] but he stubbornly refused to conserve his resources. Perhaps the supreme irony of his life was that, after striving so long and so hard to break out from the underworld of the work-beast, he succeeded in working himself to death.

CHAPTER 4

The Symbolic Wilderness

> Eastward I go only by force, but westward I go free. . . . Let me live where I will, on this side is the city, on that the wilderness, and ever I am leaving the city and more and more withdrawing into the wilderness.   —Henry David Thoreau, "Walking"

> I'd rather win a water-fight in the swimming pool, or remain astride a horse that is trying to get out from under me, than write the great American novel. Each man to his liking. . . . That is why I am building the *Snark*. I am so made. I like, that is all. The trip around the world means big moments of living.
>   —Jack London, *The Cruise of the Snark*

NOT surprisingly, water symbolism is predominant in *Martin Eden*; for the novel was written at sea during the most highly publicized of all Jack London's many wanderings. "It was all due to Captain Joshua Slocum and his *Spray,* plus our own wayward tendencies," explained Charmian. "We read him aloud to the 1905 camp children at Wake Robin Lodge, in the Valley of the Moon, as we sat in the hot sun resting between water fights and games of tag in the deep swimming pool. *Sailing Alone Around the World* was the name of the book, and when Jack closed the cover on the last chapter, there was a new idea looking out of his eyes."[1] That new idea was taking shape before the next year was out. If Joshua Slocum could sail a thirty-seven-foot sloop around the world by himself, so could Jack London—with his gritty little "mate-woman" by his side.[2]

No ingenuity nor expense would be spared in making Jack London's the finest sailing vessel of her size ever built. She would set sail from Oakland on October 1, 1906; and, though a sailboat, she would carry a rugged seventy-horsepower gasoline engine for added safety and convenience; she would be con-

124

structed of the finest buttless planking that money could buy;
with three watertight bulkheads, she would be not only un-
sinkable but virtually unleakable; she would be stocked with
six months' provisions including dozens of crates of fresh fruits
and vegetables; she would be forty-five feet long (including an
extra five feet for indoor bathroom); her beautiful bow would
defy the heaviest seas; and she would be called the *Snark* (from
Lewis Carroll's famous mock-epic).

The *Snark* was, indeed, a terrible "Boojum." Jack's careful
planning had taken into consideration neither the San Francisco earthquake of April, 1906, nor the subtler disasters of
modern industrial production standards. The *Snark*, costing over
five times the $7,000 originally calculated, did not sail until
April, 1907; before she cleared the harbor, her engine broke
loose from its bed-plate and fell on its side; she was discovered
to have multiple butts in her beautiful planking; her bottom,
her sides, and her water-tight compartments leaked; leaking
kerosene spoiled the provisions; she was two feet short; the
bathroom plumbing failed on the first day at sea; and her beautiful bow could not be made to heave to. No boat had ever
been more fatefully named.

With more courage than discretion Jack persisted in his
travel scheme and somehow managed to get the *Snark* to Hawaii,
where she underwent major repairs, and then across the Pacific
to the Marquesas, the Fijis, the Solomons, and Australia.
There, two years after embarking, bad health forced him to
abandon his circumnavigation and head for home. But, abortive
as the voyage was, the *Snark* did provide some "big moments
of living" which the veteran writer could convert to ready cash
and, occasionally, to the sounder currency of art. Perhaps most
significant from the critic's viewpoint, the *Snark* experience
served as a catalyst—much in the same way the Klondike had
done ten years before—for London's mythopoeic genius.

A critical commonplace today is that the American literary
genius from Jonathan Edwards to William Faulkner has tended
to express itself in symbolism. All major American novelists, in
this view, are Transcendental—not because they share Emerson's hearty optimism—but because they see the phenomenal
world as essentially a projection of the spiritual or psychological

world—because they posit an affinity between Nature and Soul, and because they are all, finally, moral idealists. In the case of Jack London this moral idealism—despite his protestation of materialistic monism—manifested itself principally in two ways: first, in his scientific and sociological progressivism; second, in his fictional projection of moral values onto Nature, especially onto natural settings. Both relate to the same universal pattern in that they reflect the human yearning to recapture the perfection of Eden.

This motif, the quest for Paradise, is recurrent throughout London's work, both fictional and autobiographical; his career might well be studied as a lifelong series of attempts to escape the corruptions of civilization and to recapture the simple, maternal security of Nature. The first major revelation of this archetype was the White Silence: the vast, still wilderness of the Northland Saga. There, Nature was cold, impassive, awesome; man, puny and insignificant. Even so, a cosmic orderliness existed in the harsh, immutable laws of the White Silence; and a moral certitude resulted from the country's effects upon the men who inhabited it. The unfit—the morally weak, the selfish, the foolhardy—perished. Those who survived were improved because of their adaptation to the Northland Code. The outer cold stimulated an inner warmth: men were drawn closer together in the bond of cooperation, sympathy, and brotherhood because these were the virtues necessary to survival, as were integrity, courage, forebearance, and—above all—imagination. This highest of human faculties enabled its possessor to understand the ways of the Northland so well that he could anticipate emergencies before they occurred, adapt himself to Nature's laws, and never attempt foolishly to impose the devious customs of civilization upon the inviolable wilderness. Still, the Northland was a far cry from Eden; its spiritual wellsprings were pure—but they were frozen. Although an agent of moral reformation, the region provided neither warmth nor security. Man could discover a certain serenity in the Arctic wastes, but it was the blank serenity of death. In short, it was a region to escape *from*—not *to*.

The South Seas held forth the promise of warmth, life, and new symbolic vistas.

I *Paradise Lost*

> And now all this strength and beauty has departed, and the Valley
> of Typee is the abode of some dozen wretched creatures, afflicted by
> leprosy, elephantiasis, and tuberculosis. . . . Life has rotted away in
> this wonderful garden spot, where the climate is as delightful and
> healthful as any to be found in the world. . . .
> When one considers the situation, one is almost driven to the con-
> clusion that the white race flourishes on impurity and corruption. . . .
>   —Jack London, *The Cruise of the Snark*

"This is the twentieth century, and we stink of gasoline,"
mutters Prince Akuli, the Oxford-educated gentleman whose
sole legacy from a past age rich in myth is the dry shin bone
of a great Earth-Princess three centuries dead.[3] The statement
might have been borrowed directly from T. S. Eliot but for the
fact that the first volume of this great poet's work did not appear
in print until the year after Jack London died. It may come as
a surpise to many contemporary scholars that, several years
before Eliot immortalized Miss Jessie L. Weston by poeticizing
the cruelties of April, the Wonder Boy of the Naturalist Carnival
had already discovered a similar key—perhaps the skeleton key
—to the "lost-ness" of modern man in the primitive folklore of
Polynesia—and in the writings of Carl Jung.

In the same symbolic tradition that included James Fenimore
Cooper ahead of him and William Faulkner after him, London
was acutely sensitive to the tragic consequences of the white
man's inevitable exploitation of the wilderness and his pollution
of the earth. When Jack first landed in Hawaii in 1904 en route
to the Russo-Japanese War, he thought he had found Elysium,
a paradise of flower-swept valleys peopled by bronzed youths
and golden maidens. "When Hawaii was named the Paradise
of the Pacific," he wrote afterwards, "it was inadequately named.
The rest of the Seven Seas and the islands in the midst thereof
should have been included with the Pacific. 'See Naples and
die'—they spell it differently here: *See Hawaii and live.*"[4] To
live there would be to experience the climate of Eden both
in weather and in human relations: "Hawaii and the Hawaiians
are a land and a people loving and lovable. By their language
may ye know them, and in what other land save this one is the

commonest form of greeting, not 'Good day,' nor 'How d'ye do,'
but 'Love'? That greeting is *Aloha*—love, I love you, my love
to you. Good day—what is it more than an impersonal remark
about the weather? How do you do—it is personal in a merely
casual interrogative sort of a way. But Aloha! It is a positive
affirmation of the warmth of one's own heart-giving" (279).
Hawaii and the other islands of Polynesia inspired outbursts
of lyrical description as fine as any in London's works:

> As I write these lines I lift my eyes and look seaward. I am on
> the beach of Waikiki on the island of Oahu. Far, in the azure sky,
> the trade-wind clouds drift low over the blue-green turquoise of
> the deep sea. Nearer, the sea is emerald and light olive-green. Then
> comes the reef, where the water is all slaty purple flecked with red.
> Still nearer are brighter greens and tans, lying in alternate stripes
> and showing where sandbeds lie between the living coral banks.
> Through and over and out of these wonderful colors tumbles and
> thunders a magnificent surf. As I say, I lift my eyes to all this,
> and through the white crest of a breaker suddenly appears a dark
> figure, erect, a man-fish or a sea-god, on the very forward face of
> the crest where the top falls over and down, driving in toward
> shore buried to his loins in smoking spray, caught up by the sea
> and flung landward, bodily, a quarter of a mile. It is a Kanaka
> on a surf-board. And I know that when I have finished these lines
> I shall be out in that riot of color and pounding surf, trying to bit
> those breakers even as he, and failing as he never failed, but living
> life as the best of us may live it. And the picture of that colored
> sea and that flying sea-god Kanaka becomes another reason for
> the young man to go west, and farther west, beyond the Baths of
> Sunset, and still west till he arrives home again.[5]

Polynesia also confirmed the new Jungian insights that Jack
discovered during his last year.[6] The first American fictionist
deliberately to synchronize his stories with Jung's theory of
racial memory, London exclaimed to Charmian in the summer
of 1916, "I tell you I am standing on the edge of a world so new,
so terrible, so wonderful, that I am almost afraid to look over
into it" (*Book of Jack London*, II, 323). Echoes of this brave
new world reverberate throughout "The Bones of Kahekili,"
"The Tears of Ah Kim," "When Alice Told Her Soul," "Shin
Bones," and "The Water Baby," which were written late in

his career. In the last of these stories, old Kohokumu, a garrulous Hawaiian skin diver, amuses the narrator John Lakana with his primitive folk tales; despite good-natured skepticism, Lakana (Hawaiian for "London") is entranced by the old man's recital: "Lying back with closed eyes, I lost count of time. I even forgot that Kohokumu was chanting till reminded of it by his ceasing" (*On the Makaloa Mat*, 146).

Claiming the sea as his mother, the ancient Hawaiian of "The Water Baby" discloses the archetypal symbolism which, according to Jung, emanates from man's "collective unconscious": "Why have I thought this thought of my return to my mother and of my rebirth from my mother into the sun? . . . I do not know, save that, without whisper of man's voice or printed word, without prompting from otherwhere, this thought has arisen from within me, from the deeps of me that are as deep as the sea. . . . It is of old time before me, and therefore it is true" (151). Charmian reports that "The Water Baby" was completed on October 2, 1916, the last story Jack wrote before his death, and that in his copy of Jung's work he underscored the quotation of Jesus's words to Nicodemus: "Think not carnally or thou art carnal, but think symbolically and then thou art spirit" (*Book of Jack London*, II, 354).

But, though London returned again to Hawaii in his later years literally as well as fictionally, and though a handful of his Polynesian stories rival the greatness of his best Northland tales, it was not the Eden of his dreams: it was, instead, Paradise Lost, a land whose economy had been commercialized, whose politics had been usurped, whose ecology had been upset, and whose beautiful natives had been contaminated by the "civilized" *haoles*. As the central character of the story "Koolau the Leper" remarks, "They came like lambs, speaking softly. . . . They were of two kinds. The one kind asked our permission, our gracious permission, to preach to us the word of God. The other kind asked our permission, our gracious permission, to trade with us. That was the beginning. Today all the islands are theirs, all the land, all the cattle—everything is theirs." Also theirs is the "rotting sickness" of civilization, the leprosy which has metamorphosed these lovely people into hideous monsters with stumps for arms and gaping holes for faces: "The sickness is

not ours. We have not sinned. The men who preached the word
of God and the word of Rum brought the sickness with the
coolie slaves who work the stolen land."[7]

"Koolau" is the story of a community, the inhabitants of the
Kalalau Valley on the island of Kauai, condemned to ostracism
upon Molokai because they have been stricken with leprosy.
Rather than accept the injustice of this sentence, they decide
to resist any efforts to force them from their beloved island.
As one old native, a former judge in the Hawaiian court, reasons,
"We love Kauai. Let us live here, or die here, but do not let
us go to the prison of Molokai.... I have been a judge. I know
the law and the justice, and I say to you it is unjust to steal a
man's land, to make that man sick with the Chinese sickness,
and then to put that man in prison for life" (57).

The little band fights bravely to defend its home on Kauai,
but their cause is foredoomed. Women and children, along
with the warriors, are slaughtered by the white soldiers who
come to enforce the law. Ironically, the killing occurs amidst the
idyllic beauty of the Kalalau Valley: superimposed upon the
golden backdrop of *hau* blossoms, morning glories, and papaya
fruit are the black clouds of exploding shells and the crimson
stains of broken bodies, dark metonymies of the deadly *haole*.

Demoralized by the shell-fire, the surviving lepers surrender—
all but the proud Koolau. The soldiers pursue him for six weeks
over the mountains and through the jungles of his valley—but
unsuccessfully. He either eludes them or, when cornered, out-
shoots them with his old Mauser rifle. Maimed and deformed
physically, he is indomitable spiritually—a pitiable yet magnificent rebel against the inevitable white man and the iron laws
of civilization:

Two years later, and for the last time, Koolau crawled unto [*sic*]
a thicket and lay down among the *ti*-leaves and wild ginger blossoms.
Free he had lived, and free he was dying. A slight drizzle of rain
began to fall, and he drew a ragged blanket about the distorted
wreck of his limbs. His body was covered with an oilskin coat.
Across his chest he laid his Mauser rifle, lingering affectionately for
a moment to wipe the dampness from the barrel. The hand with
which he wiped had no fingers left upon it with which to pull
the trigger. (89)

"Koolau" is representative of London's attitude toward the underdog—whether Polynesian, Klondike Indian, East End slum dweller, or American hobo. Jack was unusually touched, however, by the tragic plight of the Hawaiian leper. Hawaiian officials raised their eyebrows when Jack and Charmian celebrated the Fourth of July with the lepers on Molokai in 1907; they were scandalized by his frank, sympathetic treatment of the leprosy taboo in his Hawaiian chapters in *The Cruise of the Snark* and in his three stories "Koolau the Leper," "Good-by, Jack," and "The Sheriff of Kona."[8] But the horrors of leprosy were pale in comparison to what London encountered in the dark heart of Melanesia.

II   *Inferno*

If I were a king, the worst punishment I could inflict on my enemies would be to banish them to the Solomons. On second thought, king or no king, I don't think I'd have the heart to do it.

—Jack London, *The Cruise of the Snark*

If Polynesia was Paradise Lost, Melanesia was Hell. The conglomeration of tropical ailments suffered by London and his crew in Melanesia finally sent them packing back home in full rout, thereby cutting short the projected world tour of the *Snark*. Jack was drawing directly from personal experience when he wrote that in Melanesia "fever and dysentary are perpetually on the walk about, . . . loathsome skin diseases abound, . . . the air is saturated with a poison that bites into every pore, cut, or abrasion and plants malignant ulcers, [and] many strong men who escape dying there return as wrecks to their own countries."[9] Melanesia, not the Klondike, inspired London's bitterest Naturalistic writing; and in it the wilderness-as-Eden symbol is wholly inverted.

The deity who presides over this putrescent waste land is the Prince of Blackness himself; and the cannibalistic Melanesians are his myrmidons—"a wild lot, with a hearty appetite for human flesh and a fad for collecting human heads," London remarks in "The Terrible Solomons." "Their highest instinct of sportsmanship is to catch a man with his back turned and to smite him a cunning blow with a tomahawk that severs the spinal column at the base of the brain. It is equally true that on some islands, such as Malaita, the profit and loss account of social intercourse is calculated in homicides. Heads are a medium of exchange, and white heads are extremely valuable. Very often a dozen villages make a jack-pot, which they fatten moon by moon, against the time when some brave warrior presents a white man's head, fresh and gory, and claims the pot" (*South Sea Tales*, 199-200).

The moral effect of this rotting green hell is the exact opposite of the Northland Code. Rather than bringing out the best in those who survive, the Melanesian jungles bring out the worst. In the midst of ruthless savagery, the white man in Melanesia is reduced to like savagery; instead of escaping from corruption when he enters this wilderness, he finds himself infected by a malaise more pernicious than that of civilization. The theme of dissolution—moral as well as physical—recurs time and again in London's Melanesian fiction. "Oh, I don't mind being caught in a dirty trick," confesses one of his degenerates in *A Son of the Sun*; "I've been in the tropics too long. I'm a sick man, a damn sick man. And the whiskey, and the sun, and the fever have made me sick in morals, too. Nothing's too mean and low for me now, and I can understand why the niggers eat each other, and take heads, and such things. I could do it myself. . . . I'd as soon shoot you as smash a cockroach."[10] Life is without worth or meaning; human beings are reduced to things; brutality and killing have become a game. Thematically, much of this is reminiscent of Joseph Conrad's tropical fiction; but in tone and style it is a remarkable forecast of Ernest Hemingway:[11]

"The niggers spread out and headed for the shore, swimming. The water was carpeted with bobbing heads, and I stood up, as in a dream, and watched it all—the bobbing heads and the heads that ceased to bob. Some of the long shots were magnificent. Only one man reached the beach, but as he stood up to wade ashore, Saxtorph got him. It was beautiful. And when a couple of niggers ran down to drag him out of the water, Saxtorph got them, too.

"I thought everything was over then, when I heard the rifle go off again. A nigger had come out of the cabin companion on the run for the rail and gone down in the middle of it. The cabin must have been full of them. I counted twenty. They came up one at a

time and jumped for the rail. But they never got there. It reminded
me of trapshooting. A black body would pop out of the companion,
bang would go Saxtorph's rifle, and down would go the black
body. Of course, those below did not know what was happening
on deck, so they continued to pop out until the last one was
finished off."   (*South Sea Tales*, 250–51)

This writing is Naturalism with a vengeance. Additional intima-
tions of the "new prose" are evident in the casual underplaying
of human suffering described in "The Jokers of New Gibbon":

"It *is* a devil island, and old Koho is the big chief devil of them all.
. . . I remember six years ago, when I landed there in the British
cruiser. The niggers cleared out for the bush, of course, but we
found several who couldn't get away. One was his latest wife. She
had been hung up by one arm in the sun for two days and nights.
We cut her down, but she died just the same. And staked out in
the fresh running water, up to their necks, were three more women.
All their bones were broken and their joints crushed. The process
is supposed to make them tender for eating. They were still alive.
Their vitality was remarkable. One woman, the oldest, lingered
nearly ten days."   (*A Son of the Sun*, 137–38)

It is possible for the white man to survive in this tropical
Inferno—only by becoming worse than the natives themselves;
those same virtues essential to his survival in the Northland—
brotherhood and imagination—become fatal liabilities in
Melanesia:

A man needs only to be careful—and lucky—to live a long time in
the Solomons; but he must also be of the right sort. He must have
the hall-mark of the inevitable white man stamped upon his soul. . . .
He must have a certain grand carelessness of odds, a certain colossal
self-satisfaction, and a racial egotism that convinces him that one
white man is better than a thousand niggers every day in the week,
and that on Sunday he is able to clean out two thousand niggers.
For such are the things that have made the white man inevitable.
Oh, and one other thing—the white man who wishes to be inevitable,
must not merely despise the lesser breeds and think a lot of himself;
he must also fail to be too long on imagination. He must not understand too well the instincts, customs, and mental processes of the

blacks, the yellows, and the browns; for it is not in such fashion
that the white race has tramped its royal road around the world.
                                              (*South Sea Tales*, 200–201)

Critics who have classified London as an unmitigated pro-
ponent of "the white man's burden" have missed the calculated
irony in such passages as the foregoing.[12] It is true, of course, that
London was a bundle of contradictions in such matters—and
nothing illustrates these ambivalences better than his South Sea
tales—but the fact remains that, in his better moods, he was
anything but blind to the immoral stupidities of the white race
in its treatment of darker-skinned peoples. Regardless of London's
own peculiar brand of racism—and there can be no avoiding its
ugly implications—the sad historical fact is that many of the
leading "scientific" thinkers of his age embraced various doctrines
of white supremacy and that millions of decent Americans bought
books which blatantly preached "racial egotism" and taught their
readers to "despise the lesser breeds."

Occasionally, London's dark irony assumes the form of a grim
poetic justice in his Melanesian tales, as in the story "Mauki."
The protagonist is an inversion of the stereotyped hero: "He
weighed one hundred and ten pounds. His hair was kinky and
negroid, and he was black. He was peculiarly black. He was
neither blue-black nor purple-black, but plum-black. His name
was Mauki, and he was the son of a chief" (*South Sea Tales*, 83).
His appearance belies his sinister heroism: "There was no
strength nor character in the jaws, forehead, and nose. In the
eyes only could be caught any hint of the unknown quantities
that were so large a part of his make-up and that other persons
could not understand. These unknown quantities were pluck,
pertinacity, fearlessness, imagination, and cunning; and when
they found expression in some consistent and striking action,
those about him were astounded" (86-87).

Mauki's antagonist is Max Bunster, a hulking, psychopathic
German whose principal delight is beating cripples, old men,
and defenseless blacks. Bunster symbolizes the inevitable white
man at his degenerate worst: "Semi-madness would be a chari-
table statement of his condition. He was a bully and a coward,
and a thrice-bigger savage than any savage on the island. Being
a coward, his brutality was of the cowardly order" (103).

"Mauki," a racial chiaroscuro, presents a dramatic tableau of the white man's sadistic cruelty juxtaposed against the black man's primitive capacities for endurance and revenge. Theirs is an unwholesome "marriage" like that of Black Leclère and Bâtard in London's early Klondike story: "For better or worse, Bunster and he were tied together. Bunster weighed two hundred pounds. Mauki weighed one hundred and ten. Bunster was a degenerate brute. But Mauki was a primitive savage. While both had wills and ways of their own" (106). Bunster finds many ways to torment the black—depriving him of his tobacco allowance, beating his head against the wall, knocking out his teeth, "vaccinating" him with the live end of a cigar, for example; but his most ingenious method of torture is "caressing" his servant with a mitten made of ray-fish skin: "The skin of a shark is like sandpaper, but the skin of a ray fish is like a rasp. In the South Seas the natives use it as a wood file in smoothing down canoes and paddles. . . . The first time he tried it on Mauki, with one sweep of the hand it fetched the skin off his back from neck to armpit. Bunster was delighted" (111).

Mauki endures this treatment for week after week, but his chance for retribution finally comes when Bunster is stricken with a severe case of black-water fever. After the worst of the illness has passed, leaving the white man bedridden, Mauki carefully provisions a boat for his escape and then returns to bid farewell to his tormentor:

The house deserted, he entered the sleeping-room, where the trader lay in a doze. Mauki first removed the revolvers, then placed the ray fish mitten on his hand. Bunster's first warning was a stroke of the mitten that removed the skin the full length of his nose.

"Good fella, eh?" Mauki grinned, between two strokes, one of which swept the forehead bare and the other of which cleaned off one side of his face. "Laugh, damn you, laugh." . . .

When Mauki was done, he carried the boat compass and all the rifles and ammunition down to the cutter, which he proceeded to ballast with cases of tobacco. It was while engaged in this that a hideous, skinless thing came out of the house and ran screaming down the beach till it fell in the sand and mowed and gibbered under the scorching sun. Mauki looked toward it and hesitated. Then he went over and removed the head, which he wrapped in a mat and stowed in the stern-locker of the cutter. (115–16)

The irony is dark but clear: Bunster has paid for his moral callousness by having his thick hide removed entirely, and his sadistic head has become the trophy of its principal victim.

If Melanesia can be said to have had any salutary effect on Jack London, it was perhaps to convince him that the Eden he sought was not halfway round the globe but in his own backyard. "I also have a panacea," he confessed after suffering through the hellish ailments inflicted on him and his crew by the tropics. "It is California. I defy any man to get a Solomon Island sore in California."[13]

III *The Valley of the Moon*

The two principal ideas . . . —the negative doctrine that civilization is wicked and the positive doctrine that untouched nature is a source of strength, truth, and virtue—occur sporadically in writing about the Wild West far into the nineteenth century.

—Henry Nash Smith, *Virgin Land*

On May 26, 1905, London wrote to George P. Brett, "For a long time I have been keeping steadily the idea in mind of settling down somewhere in the country. I am in a beautiful part of California now, and I have my eyes on several properties, one of which I intend to buy, so I want to know how much money I possess in order to know to what extent I may buy" (*Letters from Jack London,* 170). The letter was postmarked at Glen Ellen, a quiet hamlet nestled in the Sonoma Valley fifty-five miles north of San Francisco. Two weeks later Jack again wrote to Brett to tell him that he had bought the Hill Ranch a half-mile from Glen Ellen: "There are 130 acres in the place, and they are 130 acres of the most beautiful, primitive land to be found in California. There are great redwoods on it, some of them thousands of years old—in fact, the redwoods are as fine and magnificent as any to be found anywhere outside the tourist groves. Also there are great firs, tan-bark oaks, maples, live-oaks, white-oaks, black-oaks, madrono and manzanita galore. There are canyons, several streams of water, many springs, etc., etc. In fact, it is impossible to really describe the place" (*Letters from Jack London,* 174).

Jack spent the next eleven years developing his "Beauty

Ranch" into one of the finest model farms in the state. Moreover, it became the model for his fourth major version of the symbolic wilderness. The California wilderness figures as the setting in a score of London's stories and eight of his novels: *White Fang, The Iron Heel, Burning Daylight, The Abysmal Brute, The Valley of the Moon, The Little Lady of the Big ,House, Jerry of the Islands,* and *Michael Brother of Jerry*.[14]

His problem, as London saw it, was how to place man in the wilderness, to enable him to live in nature and partake of its wholesome essence without contaminating the crystal springs from which he drank. This problem did not present itself in the other three versions of wilderness: in the Northern wilderness, those springs were frozen; in the tropics, they were already polluted. In the American West, however, they were both accessible and pure, a prime requisite for his Eden: it must be tractable as well as virginal—it must be, above all, benevolent toward man. Yet, man must be spiritually purified *before* entering the wilderness; he must rid himself of all selfish materialistic motives. After undergoing a spiritual cleansing of the baser motives of civilization—in short, being reborn—he could impose social refinements and scientific methods upon nature—so long as these improved the wilderness without desecrating it. Finally, man must become a self-appointed guardian of the wilderness, protecting it against all attempts to exploit and despoil. As a result of these considerations, London's fiction about the American wilderness assumes qualities of the pastoral romance necessarily alien to the White Silence and Melanesia.

London's first two novels depicting the American wilderness contrast it dramatically with the Northern wilderness. *White Fang* (1906), in its opening and concluding passages, illustrates this contrast clearly; London begins the novel with one of his most compelling descriptions of the Northland's cold hostility:

Dark spruce forest frowned on either side of the frozen waterway. The trees had been stripped by a recent wind of their white covering of frost, and they seemed to lean toward each other, black and ominous, in the fading light. A vast silence reigned over the land. The land itself was a desolation, lifeless, without movement, so lone and cold that the spirit of it was not even that of sadness. There was a hint in it of laughter, but of a laughter more terrible

than any sadness—a laughter that was mirthless as the smile of
the Sphinx, a laughter cold as the frost and partaking of the grimness of infallibility. It was the masterful and incommunicable wisdom
of eternity laughing at the futility of life and the effort of life.
It was the Wild, the savage, frozen-hearted Northland Wild. (1)

An oppressive sense of doom hovers over this wilderness: a land
of stasis and death, it is inimical not only to man but to all
life forms.

The pastoral wilderness of the American version is radically
different: "There was plenty of food and no work in the Southland, and White Fang lived fat and prosperous and happy."
The rural Elysium into which White Fang moves at the end of
the novel is a place of love and humanity. But its serenity is
vulnerable; and it must be protected from the evils of urban
society, epitomized dramatically by Jim Hall, the escaped convict
who invades Judge Scott's ranch to kill the man who sentenced
him. By saving the Judge's life, White Fang proves his right
to Edenic privilege and is consequently christened "Blessed
Wolf." Having earned this right to live in the pastoral wilderness, White Fang settles down to its softly modulated rhythms;
and the novel concludes with its hero drowsing comfortably in
the life-giving California sun while the new-born puppies he has
fathered romp around him.

The Northland-Southland polarity also provides the structural
basis for *Burning Daylight*, published in 1910. In contrast with
White Fang, this novel places emphasis upon man's heroic stature
rather than upon his puny insignificance amid the crushing
forces of the White Silence. London's description of the rowdy
recreation of the Alaskan frontiersmen illustrates this difference:
"... men have so behaved since the world began, feasting,
fighting, and carousing, whether in the dark cave-mouth or by
the fire of the squatting-place, in the palaces of imperial Rome
and the rock strongholds of robber barons, or in the sky-aspiring
hotels of modern times and in the boozing kens of sailor-town.
Just so were these men, empire builders in the Arctic night,
boastful and drunken and clamorous, winning surcease for a
few wild moments from the grim reality of their heroic toil.
Modern heroes they, and in nowise different from the heroes
of old time."[15]

And the greatest of these heroes is Elam Harnish, whose given name is an anagram for "male" and who is nicknamed "Burning Daylight." The life-force pulses so powerfully in him that he is a match even for the terrible rigors of the Northland:

Desire for mastery was strong in him, and it was all one whether wrestling with the elements themselves, with men, or with luck in a gambling game. . . . Deep in his life-processes Life itself sang the siren song of its own majesty, ever awhisper and urgent, counselling him that he could achieve more than other men, win out where they failed, ride to success where they perished. It was the urge of Life healthy and strong, unaware of frailty and decay, drunken and sublime complacence, ego-mad, enchanted by its own mighty optimism. (61)

But, even with all his strength and his egotism, Harnish is pure and simple, a true child of the wilderness.

After accumulating a large fortune in gold, this Klondike superman leaves the Northland to seek new challenges in the civilized Southland, which to his naive eyes appears to be only superficially different from the North: "It was another kind of wilderness, that was all; and it was for him to learn the ways of it, the signs and trails and water-holes where good hunting lay, and the bad stretches of field and flood to be avoided" (123). But he discovers that the jungle of big business and high finance is far more savage than the Arctic wilds. After being mulcted of his eleven million dollars by a group of smooth-talking robber barons, Harnish sees civilization in a harsh new light. He manages to recoup his fortune and succeeds in becoming a high-powered business titan but, in doing so, he undergoes a dramatic moral change:

Daylight's coming to civilization had not improved him. True, he wore better clothes, had learned slightly better manners, and spoke better English. . . . But he had hardened, and at the expense of his old-time, whole-souled geniality. Of the essential refinements of civilization he knew nothing. . . . Power had its effect on him that it had on all men. Suspicious of the big exploiters, despising the fools of the exploited herd, he had faith only in himself. This led to an undue and erroneous exaltation of his ego, while kindly consideration of others—nay, even simple respect—was destroyed, until naught was left for him but to worship at the shrine of self. (180)

His moral decay is manifested in his corresponding physical degeneration: "Physically, he was not the man of iron muscles who had come down out of the Arctic.... The old effect of asceticism, bred of terrific hardships and toil, had vanished; the features had become broader and heavier, betraying all the stigmata of the life he lived, advertising the man's self-indulgence, harshness, and brutality" (180-81). Finally, there is his tendency toward alcoholism, a disease which London commonly associates with moral and physical degeneration.

Harnish is saved through woman's love and the wilderness. Love is provided by his secretary, Dede Mason, who converts him from driving automobiles to riding horses.[16] After several wilderness meetings, Daylight proposes marriage only to be rejected because of his money: "I would dearly like to marry you, but I am afraid," Dede explains. "You would not be free for me. Your money possesses you, taking your time, your thoughts, your energy, everything, bidding you go here and go there, do this and do that. Don't you see? Perhaps it's pure silliness, but I feel that I can love much, give much—give all; and in return, though I don't want all, I want much—and I want much more than your money would permit you to give me" (291-92).

Only by renouncing his wealth and the corrupt life of the city may Harnish achieve his salvation. London implies that such a renunciation is a religious act in his description of the pastoral wilderness itself; Daylight is vaguely aware of this when he first wanders into the Valley of the Moon:

> He halted his horse, for beside the spring uprose a wild California lily. It was a wonderful flower, growing there in the cathedral nave of lofty trees.... Daylight had never seen anything like it. Slowly his gaze wandered from it to all that was about him. He took off his hat, with almost a vague religious feeling. This was different. No room for contempt and evil here. This was clean and fresh and beautiful—something he could respect. It was like a church. The atmosphere was one of holy calm. Here man felt the prompting of nobler things. (184)

Caught in the spirit of the place, Harnish is prompted by a strange compulsion to ascend Sonoma Mountain—a climb which inspires him with a new and unaccustomed spiritual exhilaration:

It was as though he were going through a sort of cleansing bath. No room here for all the sordidness, meanness, and viciousness that filled the dirty pool of city existence. Without pondering in detail upon the matter at all, his sensations were of purification and uplift. Had he been asked to state how he felt, he would merely have said that he was having a good time; for he was unaware in his self-consciousness of the potent charm of nature that was percolating through his city-rotted body and brain—potent, in that he came of an abysmal past of wilderness dwellers, while he was himself coated with but the thinnest rind of crowded civilization. (188)

Significantly, the two forces of love and the wilderness combine to effect Daylight's salvation. Dede Mason, a displaced woodland spirit like Rima of W. H. Hudson's *Green Mansions,* serves as priestess-guide for Elam:

. . . through her he came to a closer discernment and keener appreciation of nature. She showed him colors in the landscape that he would never have dreamed were there. . . . Once they rode out on a high hill brow where wind-blown poppies blazed about their horses' knees, and she was in an ecstasy over the lines of the many distances. Seven, she counted, and he, who had gazed on landscapes all his life, for the first time learned what a "distance" was. After that, and always, he looked upon the face of nature with a more seeing eye, learning a delight of his own in surveying the serried ranks of the upstanding ranges, and in slow contemplation of the purple summer mists that haunted the languid creases of the distant hills. (247)

Awakened to the pastoral beauties of the Valley of the Moon and to the elevating sensations of his first love, Daylight finally renounces his thirty-million-dollar fortune, rejects alcohol, and moves into the wilderness. His transformation, like White Fang's, reinforces Hector St. John Crèvecœur's famous dictum that "men are like plants; the goodness and flavor of the fruit proceeds from the peculiar soil and exposition in which they grow." London echoes these words in describing Elam's new birth under the combined influences of love and the wilderness: "For of all his delights in the new life, Dede was his greatest. As he explained to her more than once, he had been afraid of love all his life only in the end to come to find it the greatest thing in the world. Not alone were the two well mated, but in coming to live on the ranch they had selected the best soil in which their love would prosper" (350).

London's treatment of the wilderness theme in *The Abysmal Brute* and in *The Valley of the Moon* is essentially the same as in *White Fang* and in *Burning Daylight*. Pat Glendon, hero of *The Abysmal Brute*, is a prize-fighter who, after exposing the brutal corruption of civilization as epitomized by the boxing racket, retires with his new bride to the good life of the California wilderness.[17] Similarly, Billy Roberts—also a boxer—and Saxon Brown, the principals of *The Valley of the Moon*, find their salvation amid the healing elements of the Sonoma wilderness after their marriage has nearly collapsed in strike-ridden Oakland. The city-wilderness antithesis is reflected in Saxon's meditations after the stillbirth of her child and the jailing of her husband during the teamster strike:

> She sat there, racking her brain, the smudge of Oakland at her back, staring across the bay at the smudge of San Francisco. Yet the sun was good; the wind was good, as was the keen salt air in her nostrils; the blue sky, flecked with clouds, was good. All the natural world was right, and sensible, and beneficent. It was the man-world that was wrong, and mad, and horrible. Why were the stupid stupid? Was it a law of God? No; it could not be. God had made the wind, the air, and sun. The man-world was made by man, and a rotten job it was. (254)

Like the Harnishes, the Robertses succeed in recapturing Eden in the Valley of the Moon; and, as in the case of *White Fang*, their rebirth is confirmed when they are christened "You blessed children" by the ancient priest of the wilderness, Edmund Hale. The novel concludes with an additional promise of new life in Saxon's announcement of her pregnancy as she and Billy, standing symbolically beside a quiet pool in the heart of their canyon, gaze serenely upon a doe and new-born fawn at the edge of the forest.

In March, 1913, a few days before the first installment of *The Valley of the Moon* appeared in *Cosmopolitan*, London wrote to Editor Roland Phillips that he had just got "a splendid motif" for a new novel in hand, featuring "Three characters only—a mighty trio in a mighty situation, in a magnificently beautiful environment enhanced by all the guts of sex, coupled with strength." His three main characters were not to be "puling weaklings and moralists," he continued. "They are cultured, modern, and at the same time profoundly primitive." Waxing more enthusiastic, Jack ventured that this book would be "what I have been working toward all my writing life.... Except for my old-time punch, which will be in it from start to finish, it will not be believed that I could write it—it is so utterly fresh, so absolutely unlike anything I have ever done.... It will be a cleancut gem, even in serial form—a jewel of artistry" (*Letters from Jack London*, 374–75). So far did the author's reach exceed his grasp that we need an editorial footnote to recognize *The Little Lady of the Big House* from his prospectus. If he had been mindful of his bad luck with love trios,[18] Jack might have known better—but try again he did, with the added misfortune of deluding himself into thinking he had written a great novel.

Although Clell Peterson may be right in suggesting that *The Little Lady of the Big House* is the worst novel Jack London ever wrote,[19] it is nonetheless an interesting book. An unmistakable personal element appears in the novel: its central characters, symbolically named Dick and Paula Forrest, are modeled after Jack and Charmian London; and their efficient, scientific ranch resembles in many ways Beauty Ranch. Unlike the other works of London's pastoral wilderness, however, *The Little Lady* is darkened by an undercurrent of irony and by an atmosphere of decadence, both of which seem to have been largely unconscious.[20] Outwardly, the Forrests look like the All-American couple. Splendid physical specimens—dynamic, amiable, sensitive, fun-loving, intelligent, and tremendously appreciative of each other's virtues—they live in a beautiful home and are apparently secure in the love of friends and in the fruitfulness of nature. Yet, despite an idyllic aura, things are not quite right on the Forrest ranch: Paula is a chronic insomniac, Dick sleeps with a loaded .44 Colt automatic at his bedside, and—though he is a scientific breeder of prize stock—his own marriage is barren.

Because the Forrests themselves have no children, the theme of natural fecundity which permeates the book assumes a pathological undertone. Dick reiterates this motif obsessively in his

pagan chant, "The Song of Mountain Lad" (the Forrests' prize
stud): "Hear me! I am Eros. I stamp upon the hills. I fill the
wide valleys. The mares hear me, and startle, in quiet pastures;
for they know me. The grass grows rich and richer, the land is
filled with fatness, and the sap is in the trees. It is the spring.
The spring is mine. I am monarch of my kingdom of the spring.
The mares remember my voice. They know me aforetime through
their mothers before them. Hear me! I am Eros. I stamp upon
the hills, and the wide valleys are my heralds, echoing the sound
of my approach."[21]

Though capable of fostering procreation in nature, the Forrests themselves are sterile. Ostensibly their marriage is broken
up by Evan Graham, Dick's best friend, who falls in love with
Paula; more subtly, the breach has already been made by the
Forrests' inability to become parents. Dick contemplates suicide
when he discovers his wife's attachment to Graham; but, before
he can carry out his plan, Paula shoots herself. Her dying words
are, "I'm sorry there were no babies, Red Cloud" (391). The
suppressed irony breaks through in harsh mockery at last: "After
a long time, she sighed faintly, and began so easily to go that
she was gone before they guessed. From without, the twittering
of the canaries bathing in the fountain penetrated the silence
of the room, and from afar came the trumpeting of Mountain
Lad and the silver whinny of the Fotherington Princess" (392).

As the last novel in which London dealt with the American
wilderness as Eden, *The Little Lady* is a disappointing, distressing book. It is disappointing not only because the author prom-
ised so much more than he delivered but also because the
work itself has so much unfulfilled potential. If London had
hewed to the theme of agronomy, of successfully uniting machine
and garden through the loving application of scientific knowledge
for purposes of redemption rather than exploitation—in other
words, if London had remained true by dramatizing in his novel
the very thing he himself was doing with Beauty Ranch—*The
Little Lady* might have been a significant book, particularly in
the light of modern ecology. It might also have been a better
book artistically. Instead, he made the same mistake he had
made ten years before in writing *The Sea-Wolf*: he let his sentimental anima overcome his better artistic instinct. His "Little

Lady" is, in consequence, only Maud Brewster with a riding crop.

The Little Lady of the Big House is a distressing book not so much because of the author's wilful blindness to its artistic short-comings, however, as because of the critic's temptation to inter-pret the novel as evidence of the failure of the author's agrar-ian dream, a dream which, in the light of considerable evidence, seems to have lost little of its intensity during his last years.[22] The well-known "biographical fallacy"—the confusion of fact and fiction in relating an author's works to his personal life—is a common critical trap; but London's critics have been uncom-monly prone to fall into it. For example, on the basis of his confession in *John Barleycorn* that he drank heavily, they have inferred that he was a chronic alcoholic. Yet his drinking did not interfere with his steady thousand-words-a-day writing sched-ule, or with his carrying on the business of the Ranch, or with his playing host to the steady stream of visitors who came to the Ranch. On the basis of Paula Forrest's death, they have deduced that Jack was unconsciously trying to kill off Charmian. Yet there is solid evidence that he loved his wife deeply and loyally.[23] And on the basis of the recurrence of suicides in his fiction, they have concluded that he took his own life with an overdose of drugs on the night of November 21, 1916. But there is no real evidence of such intentions, and his last composition was not the conventional suicide note—but a letter to his daugh-ter Joan making plans for a Sunday outing with her and her younger sister Becky.[24]

The truth is, Jack London was an exceedingly complex indi-vidual, and we have not yet taken his full measure. It would there-fore seem the better part of wisdom for those of us inclined to view our literary figures through Existentialist lenses to take a fresh look at our evidence. We might begin by examining a letter London wrote in reply to one of his fans who had just read *The Little Lady of the Big House* and who was fearful that the pessimistic undertone in the novel was a reflection of the author's own philosophical outlook; Jack explains:

I assure you in reply to your question, that after having come through all of the game of life, and of youth, at my present mature age of thirty-nine years I am firmly and solemnly convinced that the game is worth the candle. I have had a very fortunate life, I have been luckier than many hundreds of millions of men in my generation have been lucky, and, while I have suffered much, I have lived much, seen much, and felt much that has been denied to the average man. Yes, indeed, the game is worth the candle. . . .

(Letters from Jack London, 461)

CHAPTER 5

A Man for Almost All Literary Seasons

Had I a thousand lives to live, I should like to have one of those lives for the exercise of the critical function. It is a snap. It is to do nothing! It is to look on. It is to hum and haw and weigh and measure, and, if you please, criticize.

—Jack London to Philo Buck[1]

IN 1936, twenty years after Jack London's death, critic Arthur Hobson Quinn wrote London's literary epitaph: "It is almost certain that his vogue is passing, for there is something impermanent in the very nature of the literature of violence."[2] That much of the world's great literature was "literature of violence" had momentarily slipped Professor Quinn's mind. Critics of the succeeding generation—New Critics, they were called—were quite willing to see London buried and forgotten: because they were attuned to the exquisite sensibility of Henry James, to the fine cerebral verse of T. S. Eliot, and to the psycholinguistic complexities of James Joyce, London seemed an insufferable boor. His name was therefore discreetly expunged from college textbooks, and he was reduced to a sentence or two in the literary histories.

He might have been forgotten entirely, except for a couple of nagging reminders: Jack London titles kept selling on the popular market, and a handful of academic critics refused to subscribe to the New Critical gentility. Even during the 1950's, at the crest of the New Critical wave, while most sensible graduate students devoted their interpretive energies to established figures like Crane, Hemingway, and Faulkner, a half-dozen critical apostates gave London the obscure immortality of *Dissertation Abstracts*.[3] By the 1960's, however, the academic climate had begun to change; and major publications by King Hendricks and Irving Shepard, Hensley Woodbridge, and Franklin Walker prepared the way for a Jack London revival.

147

That revival now appears to be in full swing. The number of London editions in *Books in Print* has virtually doubled during the past decade. Where the 1961 annual MLA bibliography listed only two London entries, the 1971 edition listed twenty-two. And three separate periodicals devoted to London are now being published.[4] In short, London's reputation seems at last secure, and the critic's job is to account for that reputation.

II *His Significance*

In spite of his immense popularity in America and abroad, Jack London's work is of minor importance in the development of our modern fiction.
                    —Harlan Hatcher, *Creating the Modern American Novel*

There is no gainsaying the genuine weaknesses in London's fiction. He can seldom sustain a long narrative structure. His best novels are occasionally marred by didacticism and sentimentalism. His female characters tend to be too flat, and his heroes are often too tall. Though he exalted content over form, he was too busy to be a philosopher; and he could seldom grasp a new idea without squeezing it into dogma. Compared with the great fictionists in American literature, London appears consistently lacking. He lacks the innovative brilliance of Poe, the encyclopedic vision of Melville, the great tragi-comic scope of Twain, the psychological sensitivity of James, the cultural responsibleness of Howells, the penetrating social insight of Fitzgerald, the stylistic integrity of Hemingway, and the magnificent artistic insouciance of Faulkner. Judged by their standards, his work does, indeed, seem to be "of minor importance in the development of our modern fiction."

However, the New Critical hegemony fell into fragments a decade ago because it could not measure the writer by any other than its own narrow rule. In the more tolerant 1970's it has become commonplace that no great writer can be accurately gauged by his shortcomings. A proper assessment of Jack London's work must therefore focus on his palpable achievements, which may be summarized as follows:

1. THE SOCIAL CRUSADER. He was a "born protestant." Writing for the working class directly from his own experiences, he

spoke with authority about the "Submerged Tenth." He was the first writer to depict the hobo with genuine understanding.[5] He also pioneered in the sympathetic, realistic treatment of the convict. Such works as *The People of the Abyss* and *The Road* possess social and historical significance apart from any literary considerations. The same may be said of much of London's fantasy and "social science fiction"—*e.g., The Iron Heel* and *The Star Rover.* As often happens with dystopian fiction, London's apocalyptic prophecies may have been self-defeating in that most of the social ills he decried have been subsequently remedied. His protests against the enormities perpetrated by capitalist overlords sound as foreign to modern America as the term "proletarian" itself. Nevertheless, the social and economic inequities he attacked were as immediate to his age as pollution and the demands of the Third World are to our own. And some of his concerns for reform—alcoholism, the rape of the wilderness, and the senselessness of the penal system—still demand our attention.

2. THE FOLK WRITER. Jack London is the archetypal "kosmos" envisioned by Walt Whitman—the poet/seer embraced as lovingly by his people as he has embraced them. He has achieved a popularity so wide and so long-standing that he seems to have become a permanent legend in the American heritage. Other popular writers have become household words in the American common culture—*e.g.,* Horatio Alger, O. Henry, Zane Grey. But in the combining of a sustained popular appeal with serious literary merit and heroic personal stature Jack London is comparable to only one other figure in American literature—Mark Twain—and even that great writer did not excite the American yearnings for romantic adventure as profoundly as London— in short, theirs are complementary appeals. London's variations on the complex theme of the American Dream place much of his work in the mainstream of our cultural history. *Martin Eden* anticipates the disenchanted success novels of Theodore Dreiser, Sinclair Lewis, and Scott Fitzgerald. *Burning Daylight* and *The Valley of the Moon* dramatize the archetypal tensions between civilization and the wilderness, the machine versus the garden.

3. THE LITERARY CRAFTSMAN. Guided by the principles of sincerity, functionalism, and imaginative Realism, London ushered in a

new prose for the modern fictionist—clear, straightforward, un-cluttered, imagistic—that is particularly well suited to the short story and to the depiction of violence and physical action. He was a major force in establishing for fiction a respectable middle ground between the gutter and the drawing room, and his efforts prepared the way for the new generations of Hemingway, Ring Lardner, and Norman Mailer.[6] A consummate storyteller, he is gifted with the power to modulate narrative tempo so that his reader is often spellbound. While even his best work suffers from stylistic lapses, even his worst work is readable. If he is sometimes clumsy, he is seldom dull. He is capable of moments of lyric intensity. He possesses, moreover, an exceptional feel-ing for irony, cosmic as well as dramatic. Such stories as "To Build a Fire" and "The Law of Life" are masterpieces of short fiction. And even such longer works as *The Sea-Wolf* and *White Fang* have become, to the embarrassment of the critics, popular classics.

But London's ultimate greatness derives from his "primor-dial vision"—the mythopoeic force which animates his finest creations and to which we respond without fully understanding why. This is the secret of the immediate and lasting appeal of a work like *The Call of the Wild,* which remains fresh and vital over the years while our critical humming and hawing grows stale.

III *His Credo*

If in the final analysis Jack London still eludes us, perhaps it is only fitting and proper. After all, he is one of our great folk heroes; and our avatars are traditionally invested with cer-tain mysteries. Perhaps, also, he himself came closest to giving us the key to the Jack London legend when he wrote:

I would rather be ashes than dust!
I would rather that my spark should burn out in a brilliant blaze
        than it should be stifled by dry-rot.
I would rather be a superb meteor, every atom of me in magnificent
        glow, than a sleepy and permanent planet.
The proper function of man is to live, not to exist.
I shall not waste my days in trying to prolong them.
I shall use my time.[7]

Notes and References

Preface

1. Max Westbrook, *Walter Van Tilburg Clark* (New York, 1969), p. 10.
2. The nineteen Jack London Scrapbooks in the Henry E. Huntington Library contain over five thousand pages of newspaper and magazine clippings about London.
3. London's books have been translated into fifty-seven languages, according to Floyd Shearer, ed., "Intelligence Report," *Parade: The Sunday Newspaper Magazine,* January 30, 1972, p. 15. London is still one of the most popular American writers in Europe, especially in the Soviet Union; see Yelena Tarkova, "What They Read," *Soviet Life,* CXCII (September, 1972), 56–57.

Chapter One

1. Dixon Wecter, *The Hero in America* (Ann Arbor, Mich., 1963), p. 16.
2. See C. T. Peterson, "The Jack London Legend," *American Book Collector,* VIII (January, 1958), 13–17; Lavon B. Carroll, "Jack London and the American Image," *American Book Collector,* XIII (January, 1963), 23–27; and Kenneth S. Lynn, *The Dream of Success* (Boston, 1955), pp. 3–10, 75–118.
3. Alfred Kazin, *On Native Grounds: An Interpretation of Modern American Prose Literature* (New York, 1942), p. 111.
4. *Letters from Jack London,* ed. King Hendricks and Irving Shepard (New York, 1965), p. 3. This letter is addressed to Mabel Applegarth, the refined young woman whom Jack had met in 1895. She became his first great love and was later used as the model for Ruth Morse in his autobiographical novel *Martin Eden.* The "twenty dollars" refers to prize money he won in a contest sponsored by the Oakland Fifth Ward Republican Club for campaign propaganda; although his article won first place and his poem second, he was never paid (the incident is fictionalized in Chapter 29 of *Martin Eden*). "Civil Exs." refers to the Civil Service examinations he had

151

taken for the position of mail carrier; *"Youth's Companion"* refers to the story "Where Boys Are Men," which was subsequently rejected.

5. Henry Steele Commager, *The American Mind: An Interpretation of American Thought and Character Since the 1880's* (New Haven, 1950): "On the one side lies an America predominantly agricultural; concerned with domestic problems; conforming, intellectually at least, to the political, economic, and moral principles inherited from the seventeenth and eighteenth centuries—an America still in the making, physically and socially; an America on the whole self-confident, self-contained, self-reliant, and conscious of its unique character and of a unique destiny. On the other side lies the modern America, predominantly urban and industrial; inextricably involved in world economy and politics; troubled with the problems that had long been thought peculiar to the Old World; experiencing profound changes in population, social institutions, economy, and technology; and trying to accommodate its traditional institutions and habits of thought to conditions new and in part alien" (p. 41).

6. Frederick Jackson Turner, "The Significance of the Frontier in American History," *The Turner Thesis Concerning the Role of the Frontier in American History*, ed. George Rogers Taylor, rev. ed. (Boston, 1956), p. 17.

7. See Sam S. Baskett, "Jack London's Heart of Darkness," *American Quarterly*, X (Spring, 1958), 77: "Enmeshed as he was in the diverse forces making up the chaotic multiplicity of twentieth-century life, inevitably London described a spiritual wasteland not far removed from Marlow's, or Kurtz's—or even [T. S.] Eliot's."

8. Franklin Walker, *Jack London and the Klondike: The Genesis of an American Writer* (San Marino, Calif., 1966), pp. 12 ff. Also see Fred Lewis Pattee, "The Prophet of the Last Frontier," in *Side-Lights on American Literature* (New York, 1922), pp. 98–160.

9. Howard Mumford Jones, *The Frontier in American Fiction: Four Lectures in the Relation of Landscape to Literature* (Jerusalem, 1956), p. 61.

10. See Roy W. Carlson, "Jack London's Heroes: A Study of Evolutionary Thought," Ph.D. Diss., University of New Mexico, 1961, pp. 6–99; and Conway Zirkle, *Evolution, Marxian Biology, and the Social Scene* (Philadelphia, 1959), pp. 318–37: e.g., "London was intellectually honest and logical, and his beliefs were always in accord with his information. He never discarded any idea of importance for the mere reason that it disturbed his tranquility or his philosophy. He was always able to change his philosophical concepts as his knowledge increased and, as long as he lived, he never ceased to grow" (320); "London was a socialist because of his belief in

aristocracy and because he saw in labor the raw material for aristocracy" (336).

Joan London, in *Jack London and His Times: An Unconventional Biography* (New York, 1939), contends that although Darwin, Spencer, Nietzsche, and Marx have been considered the major sources of London's philosophy, "these four thinkers did not influence Jack London as greatly as has been supposed," whereas the effect of Kidd's thinking, with its romantic evolutionism and its glorification of Anglo-Saxonism, "was profound" (209–12).

11. R. W. B. Lewis, *The American Adam: Innocence, Tragedy, and Tradition in the Nineteenth Century* (Chicago, 1955), p. 5.

12. Joan London, in "W. H. Chaney: A Reappraisal," *American Book Collector*, XVII (November, 1966), praises Chaney as "a man of whom Jack London need not have been ashamed" (11): "Eccentric, yes, stubborn and hot-tempered, but his excellent mind was a generous one, and his dedication to the cause of humanity, and his devotion to his principles command admiration and respect" (13).

13. *John Barleycorn* (New York, 1913), p. 41.

14. "The Apostate," *When God Laughs and Other Stories* (New York, 1911), p. 57.

15. *The Valley of the Moon* (New York, 1913), pp. 263–64.

16. *Jack London's Tales of Adventure*, ed. Irving Shepard (Garden City, N. Y., 1956), pp. 54–55.

17. *The Education of Henry Adams*, Modern Library Ed. (New York, 1931), p. 331.

18. See Samuel Eliot Morison and Henry Steele Commager, *The Growth of the American Republic*, 3rd ed. (New York, 1942), p. 331.

19. *The Road* (New York, 1907), p. 152.

20. "How I Became a Socialist," *War of the Classes* (New York, 1905), pp. 277–78.

21. Quoted in Charmian London, *The Book of Jack London* (New York, 1921), I, 210–11.

22. Pierre Berton, *The Klondike Fever: The Life and Death of the Last Great Gold Rush* (New York, 1958), p. 100.

23. Hamlin Garland, *The Trail of the Goldseekers: A Record of Travel in Prose and Verse* (1899; reprinted, New York, 1906), p. 8.

24. "The Gold Hunters of the North," *Revolution and Other Essays* (New York, 1912), p. 200.

25. Pierre Berton, "Gold Rush Writing," *Canadian Literature*, IV (Spring, 1960), 65.

26. *Jack London's Tales of Adventure*, p. 42. Compare this lyrical account of his trip with the matter-of-fact jottings in Jack's notebook, *The Book of Jack London*, I, 247–57.

Chapter Two

1. Mary Johnston, *To Have and To Hold*, Ch. XXXI, "In Which an Indian Forgives and Forgets," *The Atlantic Monthly*, LXXXV (January, 1900), 54; in this same issue appeared London's "Odyssey of the North."

2. Kenneth S. Lynn, "Disturber of Gentility" (review of Richard O'Connor's *Jack London*), *The New York Times Book Review*, February 14, 1965, p. 20.

3. This editorial decision is more comprehensible in view of the following comment in Georgia Loring Bamford, *The Mystery of Jack London: Some of His Friends, Also a Few Letters—A Reminiscence* (Oakland, Calif., 1931): "By this time there were thousands of people back from the Klondike, most of them 'busted' and, apparently, all with the feeling that they could write printable, desirable 'stuff' about the Gold Rush that would set the world on fire. Every editorial table in San Francisco was overburdened with articles and people were willing to sell them for anything they could get" (p. 111). As Clell T. Peterson observes in "Jack London's Alaskan Stories," *American Book Collector*, IX (April, 1959), 17: "It is largely true that London rose to success because of the public interest in Alaska, but he had to become a first-rate writer to do it."

4. *Letters from Jack London*, p. 8. The difficulty Jack had in collecting his five dollars is dramatized in Chapter 33 of *Martin Eden*.

5. King Hendricks, "Determination and Courage," *The Eleusis of Chi Omega*, LXVI (May, 1964), 306. Also see *Jack London Reports: War Correspondence, Sports Articles, and Miscellaneous Writings*, ed. King Hendricks and Irving Shepard (Garden City, N. Y., 1970), pp. xii–xvi.

6. Letter dated June 17, 1900, on file in the Huntington Library.

7. *The Son of the Wolf, Tales of the Far North* (Boston, 1900), p. 190.

8. In a letter to Elwyn Hoffman, October 27, 1900 (Huntington file), London wrote, ". . . there is no end of Kipling in my work. . . . I would never possibly have written anywhere near the way I did had Kipling never been." In *Jack London and His Times* (170), Joan London notes that while he was still developing his style, Jack spent days actually copying Kipling in longhand. London's defense of Kipling's art and ideas is strongly voiced in "These Bones Shall Rise Again," *Revolution and Other Essays*, pp. 219–34.

9. Maxwell Geismar, *Rebels and Ancestors: The American Novel, 1890–1915* (Boston, 1953), p. 186.

10. C. G. Jung, *Modern Man in Search of a Soul*, trans. W. S. Dell

and Cary F. Baynes, Harvest Book (New York, n.d., 1st publ. 1933), pp. 171–72.

11. See C. G. Jung, *Archetypes and the Collective Unconscious,* trans. R. F. C. Hull, 2nd ed. (Princeton, N. J., 1968), *passim.*

12. Philip Young, *Ernest Hemingway* (New York, 1952), pp. 229–30.

13. *Children of the Frost* (New York, 1902), p. 3; this entire volume of short stories is keyed to the theme of the vanishing Northland Indian; the sympathetic mood of these tales contrasts with *The God of His Fathers,* published the year before and dedicated "To the Daughters of the Wolf [the conquering Anglo-Saxon] Who Have Bred and Suckled a Race of Men."

14. Mircea Eliade, *Myth and Reality,* trans. William R. Trask (New York, 1963), p. 199.

15. James Baird, *Ishmael: A Study of the Symbolic Mode in Primitivism,* Harper Torchbook Ed. (New York, 1960), p. 334.

16. Baird mentions London several times in *Ishmael,* but always as an "exoticist" whose narratives "provide suitable examples of the Pacific voyage without the appearance of primitive feeling" (123) and whose fiction is artistically inferior to that of the genuine primitivist (37, 207). Baird rightly designates *A Son of the Sun* as a minor Nietzschean allegory; except for the first-rate story "The Pearls of Parlay," these "David Grief" stories are among London's poorest (significantly, they were the inspiration for a Hollywood TV series in the late 1950's). But he wrongly classifies this book as a "Polynesian novel": neither "Polynesian" nor "novel," it is a collection of separate, unrelated episodes set in Melanesia. In London's Polynesian and Northland fictions (none of which Baird mentions), the characteristics of authentic primitivism are clearly evident.

17. *Idle Days in Patagonia* (New York, 1917), p. 118. Note comparable instances of this phenomenon in such works as Sherwood Anderson's "Death in the Woods," Robert Frost's "Stopping by Woods on a Snowy Evening" and "Desert Places," and in Hans Castorp's venture into the heart of the Schatzalp in Thomas Mann's *Magic Mountain.*

18. *Lost Face* (New York, 1910), pp. 63–64. The holograph manuscript of this story, on file in the Huntington Library, reveals that London began by naming his protagonist "John Collins," changed to "the man" in his third paragraph, then revised his earlier references to read "the man." An unpublished computer analysis by Professor Donald Danvers, Centenary College of Louisiana, yields the following key word counts in the story: *cold* (31), *freeze*[*-ing*] (28), *frost* (10), *ice* (19), *snow* (35), *heat* (1), *hot* (2), *warmth* (4).

A full recounting of the actual episode that inspired London's story is given by Franklin Walker in *Jack London and the Klondike*, pp. 255–60.

19. "The Art of Poetry," in *Aristotle*, trans. and ed. Philip Wheelwright, enlarged ed. (New York, 1951), p. 303.

20. Herbert Muller, *The Spirit of Tragedy* (New York, 1965), pp. 1, 17. For additional commentaries on this story, *cf.* Clell T. Peterson, "The Theme of Jack London's 'To Build a Fire,'" *American Book Collector*, XVII (November, 1966), 15–18; Earle Labor and King Hendricks, "Jack London's Twice-Told Tale," *Studies in Short Fiction*, IV (Summer, 1967), 334–47 (including reprint of first version, published in *Youth's Companion*, 1902); and James K. Bowen, "Jack London's 'To Build a Fire': Epistemology and the White Wilderness," *Western American Literature*, V (Winter, 1971), 287–89.

21. Charles Child Walcutt, *American Literary Naturalism: A Divided Stream* (Minneapolis, 1956), pp. 97–98.

22. *A Daughter of the Snows* (Philadelphia, 1902), in sequence of quotes, pp. 58, 83, 201, 202, 21, 24.

23. In all fairness to London, it should be noted that this failure was not his own fault entirely. *Hearts of Three* (London, 1918; New York, 1920) was conceived as a moving-picture novel written in collaboration with the famous creator of *The Perils of Pauline*, Charles Goddard, who provided London with scenario notes. Even Charmian, often excessive in her praise, admits that the result "should be viewed as something of a joke" (see *Book of Jack London*, II, 316–19). But comedy was not one of Jack's strengths. Not only is the novel poorly written; it is marred throughout by the author's gratuitous comments about the mongrel races and his particular dislike of the Latin Americans.

24. In contrast with these fables, *Michael Brother of Jerry* (New York, 1917) is truly an animal story in that Jack wrote it as a protest against the cruelties inflicted upon animals in training them for performance on stage. (This novel is also a pioneering indictment of the inhumanity and ignorance in the treatment of lepers, especially in the United States.)

25. Alfred S. Shivers, in "The Romantic in Jack London," *Alaska Review*, I (Winter, 1963), suggests that from one point of view "the story may be taken as a misanthropic allegory in the form of a beast fable. The beast fable *per se* has its romantic basis: animals that think rationally and act under some of the same motivations that men do, therefore as heroes, and as human intelligence disguised in wolves' clothing lend to the story a sense of the wonderful and

the strange. . . . The canine hero fascinated London. . . . In the canine he could penetrate to the uttermost reaches of primitiveness, a goal toward which he seemed to be repeatedly striving" (44).

26. *The Faith of Men and Other Stories* (New York, 1904), p. 203. James Sisson has brought to my attention the German translation of "Bâtard" as "Zwei Teufel" ("Two Devils") and also the plural in the Latvian translation (see Hensley C. Woodbridge, John London, and George H. Tweney, *Jack London: A Bibliography* [Georgetown, Calif., 1966], p. 215, Item 628).

27. Joan London, *Jack London and His Times*, p. 252. *Cf.* C. G. Jung's explanation of the "primordial vision" as "an experience . . . which cannot be accepted by the conscious outlook" in *Modern Man in Search of a Soul*, p. 159.

28. Letter to George P. Brett, February 12, 1903 (Huntington file).

29. Charles G. D. Roberts, *The Kindred of the Wild* (Boston, 1902), p. 29.

30. See Simon O. Lesser, *Fiction and the Unconscious* (Boston, 1957), p. 113.

31. Maxwell Geismar, ed., "Introduction," *Jack London: Short Stories*, American Century Series (New York, 1960), pp. ix–x.

32. See Joseph Campbell, *The Hero with a Thousand Faces*, Meridian Ed. (New York, 1956), pp. 34–46.

33. Richard Chase, *The American Novel and Its Tradition*, Anchor Ed. (Garden City, N. Y., 1957), p. 13.

34. *The Call of the Wild* (New York, 1903), p. 26.

35. See J. E. Cirlot, *A Dictionary of Symbols*, trans. Jack Sage (New York, 1962), p. 223.

36. *White Fang* (New York, 1906), p. 5.

37. Quoted by George Wharton James in "Jack London, Cub of the Slums, Hero of Adventure, Literary Master, and Social Philosopher," *National Magazine*, XXXVII (December, 1912), 489–90; also quoted by Charmian London in *Book of Jack London*, II, 49–50. Also see James R. Giles, "Thematic Significance of the Jim Hall Incident in *White Fang*," *Jack London Newsletter*, II (May–August, 1969), 49–50.

38. Eliseo Vivas, *The Artistic Transaction* (Columbus, Ohio, 1963), pp. 10, 30–31.

Chapter Three

1. Granville Hicks, *The Great Tradition: An Interpretation of American Literature Since the Civil War*, rev. ed. (New York, 1935), p. 193.

2. Anna Strunsky Walling, "Memoirs of Jack London," *The Masses*, IX (July, 1917), 14.

3. Frederick J. Hoffman, *The Modern Novel in America*, Gateway Ed. (Chicago, 1954), p. 44.

4. Winifred Blatchford, "In the Library," *The Clarion* (London), No. 1304, Friday, December 1, 1916, p. 2.

5. "Getting into Print," *The Editor*, XVII (March, 1903), 82.

6. Sources in sequence: *Martin Eden* (New York, 1909), p. 232; "These Bones Shall Rise Again," *Revolution*, p. 224; "The Terrible and Tragic in Fiction," *The Critic*, XLII (June, 1903), 542, reprinted in *Jack London Reports*, p. 334; *Revolution*, pp. 231, 224; *Letters from Jack London*, p. 335.

7. "What Communities Lose by the Competitive System," in *Jack London: American Rebel*, ed. Philip Foner (New York, 1947), p. 429; originally published in *Cosmopolitan Magazine* (November, 1900).

8. "The House Beautiful," *Revolution*, p. 166.

9. Letter to Elwyn Hoffman, January 6, 1900 (Huntington file).

10. "The Phenomena of Literary Evolution," *Bookman*, XII (October, 1900), 150.

11. *Ibid.*

12. "The House Beautiful," *Revolution*, p. 170.

13. "On the Writer's Philosophy of Life," *The Occident*, LXX (December, 1916), 147, originally published in *The Editor*, October, 1899.

14. "The Material Side," *The Occident*, LXX (December, 1916), 144–45.

15. Porter Garnett, "Jack London—His Relation to Literary Art," *The Pacific Monthly*, XVII (April, 1907), 453.

16. Walling, p. 13.

17. Rose Wilder Lane quoted in Richard O'Connor, *Jack London: A Biography* (Boston, 1964), p. 139.

18. *The Kempton-Wace Letters* (New York, 1903), p. 87.

19. Jack London to Anna Strunsky, August 21, 1902 (Huntington file).

20. *The People of the Abyss* (New York, 1903), pp. 274–75. See James R. Giles, "Jack London 'Down and Out' in England: the Relevance of the Sociological Study *People of the Abyss* to London's Fiction," *Jack London Newsletter*, II (September–December, 1969), 79–83.

21. Joan London, *Jack London and His Times*, p. 250. Later, he did write again about the people of the abyss in *The Iron Heel*.

22. Roy Carlson makes a strong case in support of his assertion

that *The Sea-Wolf* was London's "most ambitious novel"—see "Jack London's Heroes: A Study of Evolutionary Thought," pp. 152 ff. Over a half-million copies of this novel have been sold in the hardcover edition by Macmillan—not including the countless paperback sales (see O'Connor, p. 198), and it has been made into eight motion pictures (see Woodbridge's *Bibliography*, pp. 282–87).

23. Quoted in Foner, pp. 61–62.

24. Robert E. Spiller, "Toward Naturalism in Fiction," *Literary History of the United States*, ed. Spiller *et al.* (New York, 1955), p. 1036; Gordon Mills, "Jack London's Quest for Salvation," *American Quarterly*, VII (Spring, 1955), 5.

25. *The Sea-Wolf* (New York, 1904), pp. 73–74.

26. James Ellis interprets Larsen's headaches as a symbol of the tension between the animal and the human in his character, and between materialism and idealism in his philosophy; see "A New Reading of *The Sea Wolf*," *Western American Literature*, II (Summer, 1967), 129–31.

27. Zirkle, p. 331. See Van Weyden's comments about Larsen as an anachronism in *The Sea-Wolf*, p. 75; see also the title story in *The Strength of the Strong* (New York, 1914), pp. 1–33.

28. Quoted in Foner, p. 61.

29. Robert Brainard Pearsall suggests that "such people may be willing to die for love [but the] notion of slipping into bed for love would not necessarily occur to them"—in "Elizabeth Barrett Meets Wolf Larsen," *Western American Literature*, IV (Spring, 1969), 12.

30. Letter to George P. Brett, January 20, 1903 (Huntington file).

31. See "Jack London to Yale Men," *Yale Alumni Weekly*, XV, 18 (January 31, 1906), 344 [my thanks to James Sisson for this reference]; also see Joan London, *Jack London and His Times*, p. 301, for a slightly different version of London's Yale speech, and pp. 308–9 for his speech to the rich New Yorkers.

32. Joseph Blotner, *The Modern American Political Novel, 1900–1960* (Austin, 1966), pp. 150–51.

33. *The Iron Heel* (New York, 1908), pp. 83–84.

34. Letter to "Dear Comrade Harris," October 26, 1914 (Huntington file).

35. See London's review of this book in *War of the Classes*, pp. 197–206.

36. Joan London, *Jack London and His Times*, p. 307.

37. Irving Stone, *Sailor on Horseback: The Biography of Jack London* (Cambridge, Mass., 1938), p. 229.

38. Spiller, p. 1037; Foner, p. 97; Geismar, p. 163; Walter Rideout, *The Radical Novel in the United States, 1900–1954* (Cambridge,

160 JACK LONDON

Mass., 1956), p. 42; Max Lerner, "Introduction," *The Iron Heel,* American Century Series (New York, 1957), p. xi.

39. In fact, at least two attempts to psychoanalyze London antedate Geismar's: Wilfrid Lay, "John Barleycorn under Psychoanalysis," *Bookman,* XIV (March, 1917), 47–54; and "Ms. Notes [on] Jung's *Psychology of the Unconscious* Compiled by Mary Wilshire lately direct from Jung in Zurich" (Huntington file). Charmian used the latter, along with Jack's marked copy of C. G. Jung's *Psychology of the Unconscious,* ed. Beatrice M. Hinkle (New York, 1916), in writing *The Book of Jack London* (II, 320–24, 334, 353–59); especially noteworthy is the suggestion that London's unconscious projected itself symbolically in the last stories he wrote, such as "The Red One": "Sometimes I wonder if it can be possible, in the ponderings of the dying scientist, Basset, that Jack London revealed more of himself than he would have been willing to admit—or else, who knows? More of himself than he himself realized," says Charmian (II, 334).

40. *Before Adam* (New York, 1907), p. 1. In writing this novel, London was influenced by the "germ plasm theory of heredity" formulated by the German biologist August Weismann; for an instructive discussion of this and related ideas, see Hamilton Cravens and John C. Burnham, "Psychology and Evolutionary Naturalism in American Thought, 1890–1940," *American Quarterly,* XXIII (December, 1971), 635–57.

41. *The Scarlet Plague* (New York, 1915), pp. 73–75. This novel was first serialized in *London Magazine,* XXVIII (June, 1912), 513–40.

42. Geismar, *Rebels and Ancestors,* p. 210; Stone, p. 311.

43. Ed. Morrell, *The Twenty-Fifth Man* (Montclair, N. J., 1924), pp. 367-68. Also see Charmian's record of Jack's response to the evidence of Morrell's ordeal, *Book of Jack London,* II, 226. London used Morrell's own story as a frame, and many of the prison episodes in *The Star Rover* are virtually identical to those depicted as fact in Morrell's book.

44. *The Star Rover* (New York, 1915), p. 122.

45. Letter to the author from William F. Almand, Jr., February 13, 1962. For a more recent testimonial to the moving power of this novel, see Jonathan Yardley, "Reconsideration: Jack London," *The New Republic,* June 2, 1973, pp. 31–33.

46. Franklin Walker, "Jack London: *Martin Eden,*" in *The American Novel from James Fenimore Cooper to William Faulkner,* ed. Wallace Stegner (New York, 1965), p. 133.

47. The *Mariposa* was the name of the ship Jack himself had sailed on when he interrupted his *Snark* cruise in 1908 to return home to straighten out his financial affairs.

48. Jung, *The Archetypes of the Collective Unconscious,* pp. 17, 177–78.

49. In a letter to George Brett of Macmillan from Papeete, Tahiti, February 27, 1908, London wrote: "You will shortly receive, by express, the manuscript of my new novel. . . . In case "SUCCESS" is already a copyrighted title, I give you herewith three titles which I prefer in the following order: (1) SUCCESS (2) STAR-DUST (3) MARTIN EDEN . . . I don't know what you will think of this novel; I don't know what to think of it myself. But at any rate, I think you will find it fresh and original" (Huntington file).

50. London allegedly took the hero's given name from Martin Johnson, the young cook and handyman aboard the *Snark,* who later became a world-famous explorer; but Anders Kruskopf, in "Martin Eden of Sonoma," *American-Scandinavian Review,* XXXI (Winter, 1943), 347–48, points out that Martin Eden was the name of one of London's neighbors.

51. A persuasive refutation of the suicide theory is Alfred S. Shivers, "Jack London: Not a Suicide," *The Dalhousie Review,* XLIX (Spring, 1969), 43–57. An expert in pharmacology, Shivers explains the futility of attempting to calculate exact lethal dosages of morphine (the alleged evidence Irving Stone used in *Sailor on Horseback* as the basis for his inference that London deliberately took his own life).

Chapter Four

1. Charmian Kittredge London, *The Log of the Snark* (New York, 1915), p. vii.

2. The actual size of his crew was six: "Uncle" Roscoe Eames, Herbert Stolz, Martin Johnson, Tochigi, Jack, and Charmian. Of the original six, only half—Martin, Jack, and Charmian—were together at the end of the voyage.

3. "Shin Bones," *On the Makaloa Mat* (New York, 1919), p. 141.

4. "From 'My Hawaiian Aloha,'" *Stories of Hawaii by Jack London,* ed. A. Grove Day (New York, 1965), p. 282.

5. *The Cruise of the Snark* (New York, 1911), pp. 58–59.

6. See James I. McClintock, "Jack London's Use of Carl Jung's *Psychology of the Unconscious,*" *American Literature,* XLII (November, 1970), 336–47; and Earle Labor, "Paradise Almost Regained," *Saturday Review,* April 3, 1965, pp. 43–44.

7. *The House of Pride* (New York, 1912), pp. 47–48, 57. This story was based on an episode in Hawaiian history in which Deputy Sheriff Louis H. Stolz (father of *Snark* crewman Bert Stolz) was killed; see A. Grove Day's "Introduction," *Stories of Hawaii,* p. 11,

and Day's *Jack London in the South Seas* (New York, 1971), pp. 80–81.

8. See Day, *Stories of Hawaii,* pp. 9–12.

9. "The Terrible Solomons," *South Sea Tales* (New York, 1911), p. 199.

10. *A Son of the Sun* (New York, 1911), pp. 17–19.

11. See especially Ernest Hemingway's *In Our Time* (New York, 1958; first publ. 1925), pp. 11–12, 33, 43. For Conrad's influence, see Sam S. Baskett, "Jack London's Heart of Darkness," *American Quarterly,* X (Spring, 1958), 66–77.

12. For additional examples of this double-edged irony, see "Chun Ah Chun," *The House of Pride,* pp. 151–89, and "The Chinago," *When God Laughs and Other Stories* (New York, 1911), pp. 153–85; also see Steven T. Dhondt, "Jack London's *When God Laughs*: Overman, Underdog, and Satire," *Jack London Newsletter,* II (May–August, 1969), 51–57.

13. *The Cruise of the Snark,* p. 276.

14. Parts of *The Iron Heel* (the hideout), *Burning Daylight, The Valley of the Moon, Jerry* and *Michael* (the endings) are set in the Sonoma Valley; *White Fang,* in the Santa Clara Valley (Buck's old home); *The Abysmal Brute,* in Siskiyou and Mendocino Counties; *The Little Lady,* in the foothills east of Sacramento. I am indebted to James Sisson for his help in locating these settings.

15. *Burning Daylight* (New York, 1910), p. 30.

16. Clell T. Peterson interprets this dramatic first encounter between Dede (gracefully on horseback) and Elam (disgracefully ditched in his car) as the turning point in the novel; "Jack London's Sonoma Novels," *American Book Collector,* IX (October, 1958), 17.

17. *The Abysmal Brute* was based on one of several plots Jack bought from Sinclair Lewis. See *Letters from Jack London,* pp. 383, 388. Also see Franklin Walker, "Jack London's Use of Sinclair Lewis Plots," *Huntington Library Quarterly,* XVII (November, 1953), 59–74.

18. See, for example, *Adventure* (1911), a warmed-over version of *A Daughter of the Snows.* The *ménage à trois* is equally unsuccessful in his later novel, *Hearts of Three* (1920).

19. Clell T. Peterson, "Jack London's Sonoma Novels," p. 15. A more favorable commentary is provided by Edwin B. Erbentraut in "The Symbolic Triad in London's *The Little Lady of the Big House*," *Jack London Newsletter,* III (September–December, 1970), 82–89.

20. See Peterson, pp. 17–20, for a perceptive analysis of the decadent sexual imagery in *The Little Lady.*

21. *The Little Lady of the Big House* (New York, 1916), pp.

84–85. London's choral play *The Acorn-Planter* (New York, 1916) also celebrates the pagan fertility theme.

22. Letters and notes on file at both the Huntington Library and the Merrill Library at Utah State University reveal that London was busily involved in developing the Ranch until the day of his death—including plans for rebuilding Wolf House and for starting a school on the Ranch.

23. See especially London's inscriptions to Charmian in the collection of signed first editions at Utah State University. In *The Little Lady of the Big House* he writes: "Dearest Mate:- The years pass. You and I pass. But yet our love abides—more firmly, more deeply, more surely, for we have built our love for each other, not upon the sand, but upon the rock." London's personal letters to Charmian reveal the same devotion.

24. *Letters from Jack London*, p. 480. Also see note 39 in *Chapter Three* above. A clue to the mystery of London's death may be found in Jungian psychology and in the application of Jung's theories to London's own writings.

Chapter Five

1. Letter dated March 1, 1913, in *Creator and Critic: A Controversy between Jack London and Philo M. Buck, Jr.*, ed. King Hendricks (Logan, Utah, 1961), p. 34. This monograph includes Buck's essay "The American Barbarian" from *The Methodist Review* (September, 1912), along with the six letters exchanged between Buck and London (two by Buck, four by London) and Hendricks's introductory essay.

2. Arthur Hobson Quinn, *American Fiction: An Historical and Critical Survey* (New York, 1936), p. 542.

3. Sam S. Baskett, "Jack London's Fiction: Its Social Milieu," Ph.D. Diss., University of California, 1951; Elsie Edmondson, "The Writer as Hero in Important American Fiction since Howells," Ph.D. Diss., University of Michigan, 1954; Robert Belton Holland, "Jack London: His Thought and Art in Relation to His Time," Diss., University of Wisconsin, 1952; Abraham Rothberg, "The House That Jack Built: A Study of Jack London: the Man, His Times, and His Works," Ph.D. Diss., Columbia University, 1952; Anne Marie Springer, "Jack London and Upton Sinclair," in "The American Novel in Germany: A Study of the Critical Reception of Eight American Novelists Between the Two World Wars," Ph.D. Diss., University of Pennsylvania, 1959; Thomas Daniel Young, "Jack London and the Era of Social Protest," Ph.D. Diss., Vanderbilt University, 1950. Also during the 1950's, a few noteworthy essays on London appeared in scholarly

publications: Sam S. Baskett, "Jack London and the Oakland Waterfront," *American Literature*, XXVII (November, 1955), 363–71, and "Jack London's Heart of Darkness," *American Quarterly*, X (Spring, 1958), 66–77; Gordon Mills, "Jack London's Quest for Salvation," *American Quarterly*, VII (Spring, 1955), 3–14, and "The Symbolic Wilderness," *Nineteenth-Century Fiction*, XIII (March, 1959), 329–40; and Charles Child Walcutt, "Jack London: Blond Beasts and Supermen," *American Literary Naturalism: A Divided Stream* (Minneapolis: University of Minnesota, 1956), pp. 87–113.

4. *Jack London Newsletter*, ed. Hensley C. Woodbridge (Southern Illinois University Library, Carbondale, Ill.); *The London Collector*, ed. Richard Weiderman (Grand Rapids, Michigan 49506); *What's New About London, Jack?*, ed. David H. Schlottmann (929 South Bay Rd., Olympia, Washington). Also noteworthy is the *American Book Collector*, ed. W. B. Thorsen (1822 School St., Chicago, Ill.), which has regularly published articles on London during the past two decades; see especially the "Jack London Special Number" of *American Book Collector*, XVII (November, 1966).

5. See Frederick Feied, *No Pie in the Sky: The Hobo as American Cultural Hero in the Works of Jack London, John dos Passos, and Jack Kerouac* (New York, 1964).

6. London virtually invented the modern prize-fight story. *The Game* (New York, 1905), in which the hero is killed in the ring, is alleged to have prompted Heavyweight Champion Gene Tunney's retirement from boxing when he read London's short novel in the late 1920's. "The Madness of John Harned," in *The Night-Born* (New York, 1913), was inspired by London's witnessing of a bull-fight in Quito, Ecuador, on his way home from the South Seas in 1909; the hero is so enraged by the torturing of the bull that he runs amuck, killing several soldiers and government officials before he is fatally wounded. Artistically superior to either of these are "A Piece of Steak" (*When God Laughs*, 1911) and "The Mexican" (*The Night-Born*), which have become classics of the Ring and which must be ranked among the dozen best stories London wrote. For a detailed treatment of London's boxing stories, see Ch. 2, "The Game," in my "Jack London's Literary Artistry: A Study of His Images and Symbols as Related to His Themes," Ph.D. Diss., University of Wisconsin, 1961, pp. 66–98. Also, compare his series on the Jeffries-Johnson bout (*Jack London Reports*, pp. 264–301) with Norman Mailer's coverage of the Frazier-Ali fight in *Life* magazine, LXX (March 19, 1971), 18–36.

7. *Jack London's Tales of Adventure*, p. vii.

Selected Bibliography

1. Original Materials

More than 16,000 partially catalogued items related to Jack London (letters, notes, manuscripts, scrapbooks) are on file at the Henry E. Huntington Library in San Marino, California. The second largest collection of Londoniana is held by the Utah State University Library in Logan. Other important collections are located at the Bancroft Library, University of California, Berkeley; the Special Collections Department of the University of California at Los Angeles; the Cresmer Collection at the University of Southern California; the Stanford University Library; the Stuart Library of Western Americana at the University of the Pacific; the Oakland Public Library; the Special Collections Library at the University of Virginia; and the Jack London Museum in Glen Ellen, California.

2. Books

At least three Jack London collected editions have been published in the Soviet Union; seventeen volumes of the *Obras completas* have been issued in Portugal; four volumes of the Bodley Head Jack London have been released in England; Horizon Press has recently published a dozen volumes edited by I. O. Evans and printed in Great Britain; Macmillan has reissued a half-dozen hardbound titles enhanced by handsome illustrations and introductory essays; and the paperback publishers have struck a bonanza as title after title has dropped out of copyright. But the scholar must often rely on cheap, sometimes inaccurate reprints or on Interlibrary Loans, realizing that some items are virtually inaccessible. The following list of scarce first editions, while a source of delight to the second-hand book dealer, represents an increasing frustration for the serious London student.

The Son of the Wolf [stories]. Boston: Houghton Mifflin, 1900.
The God of His Fathers [stories]. New York: McClure, Phillips, 1901.
Children of the Frost [stories]. New York: Macmillan, 1902.
The Cruise of the Dazzler [juvenile]. New York: Century, 1902.

A Daughter of the Snows [novel]. Philadelphia: J. B. Lippincott, 1902.
The Kempton-Wace Letters [with Anna Strunsky]. New York: Macmillan, 1903.
The Call of the Wild [novella]. New York: Macmillan, 1903.
The People of the Abyss [sociological study]. New York: Macmillan, 1903.
The Faith of Men [stories]. New York: Macmillan, 1904.
The Sea-Wolf [novel]. New York: Macmillan, 1904.
War of the Classes [essays]. New York: Macmillan, 1905.
The Game [novella]. New York: Macmillan, 1905.
Tales of the Fish Patrol. New York: Macmillan, 1905.
Moon-Face and Other Stories. New York: Macmillan, 1906.
White Fang [novel]. New York: Macmillan, 1906.
Scorn of Women [play]. New York: Macmillan, 1906.
Before Adam [novel]. New York: Macmillan, 1907.
Love of Life and Other Stories. New York: Macmillan, 1907.
The Road [tramping reminiscences]. New York: Macmillan, 1907.
The Iron Heel [novel]. New York: Macmillan, 1908.
Martin Eden [novel]. New York: Macmillan, 1909.
Lost Face [stories]. New York: Macmillan, 1910.
Revolution and Other Essays. New York: Macmillan, 1910.
Burning Daylight [novel]. New York: Macmillan, 1910.
Theft: A Play in Four Acts. New York: Macmillan, 1910.
When God Laughs and Other Stories. New York: Macmillan, 1911.
Adventure [novel]. New York: Macmillan, 1911.
The Cruise of the Snark [travel sketches]. New York: Macmillan, 1911.
South Sea Tales. New York: Macmillan, 1911.
The House of Pride and Other Tales of Hawaii. New York: Macmillan, 1912.
A Son of the Sun [stories]. Garden City, N. Y.: Doubleday, Page, 1912.
Smoke Bellew [stories]. New York: Century, 1912.
The Night-Born [stories]. New York: Century, 1913.
The Abysmal Brute [novella]. New York: Century, 1913.
John Barleycorn [autobiographical treatise]. New York: Century, 1913.
The Valley of the Moon [novel]. New York: Macmillan, 1913.
The Strength of the Strong [stories]. New York: Macmillan, 1914.
The Mutiny of the Elsinore [novel]. New York: Macmillan, 1914.
The Scarlet Plague [novella]. New York: Macmillan, 1915.
The Star Rover [novel]. New York: Macmillan, 1915.
The Acorn-Planter: A California Forest Play. New York: Macmillan, 1916.

The Little Lady of the Big House [novel]. New York: Macmillan, 1916.
The Turtles of Tasman [stories]. New York: Macmillan, 1916.
The Human Drift [miscellany]. New York: Macmillan, 1917.
Jerry of the Islands [novel]. New York: Macmillan, 1917.
Michael Brother of Jerry [novel]. New York: Macmillan, 1917.
The Red One [stories]. New York: Macmillan, 1918.
On the Makaloa Mat [stories]. New York: Macmillan, 1919.
Hearts of Three [novel]. New York: Macmillan, 1920.
Dutch Courage and Other Stories. New York: Macmillan, 1922.
The Assassination Bureau, Ltd. [novel completed by Robert L. Fish]. New York: McGraw-Hill, 1963.
Letters from Jack London, ed. King Hendricks and Irving Shepard. New York: Odyssey, 1965.
Jack London Reports [essays and newspaper articles], ed. King Hendricks and Irving Shepard. New York: Doubleday, 1970.
Daughters of the Rich [curtain raiser], ed. James E. Sisson. Oakland, Calif.: Holmes Book Co., 1971.
Gold [three-act play written in collaboration with Herbert Heron], ed. James Sisson. Oakland, Calif.: Holmes Book Co., 1972.

SECONDARY SOURCES

1. Bibliography

BUBKA, TONY. "A Jack London Bibliography: A Selection of Reports Printed in the San Francisco Bay Area Newspapers: 1896–1967." M.A. Thesis. San Jose State College, 1968.
SISSON, JAMES E. "Jack London's Plays: A Chronological Bibliography." Included in *Daughters of the Rich* (one-act play by London, edited by Sisson). Oakland, Calif.: Holmes Book Co., 1971. Lists seventeen plays, most of which were never published. Also see Sisson's "Jack London's Published Poems: A Chronological Bibliography," *The London Collector,* I (July, 1970), 20–21, which lists twelve items. These two lists complement Woodbridge.
WALKER, DALE L., and JAMES E. SISSON III. *The Fiction of Jack London; A Chronological Bibliography.* El Paso: Texas Western Press, 1972. Annotated, with photographs.
WOODBRIDGE, HENSLEY C., JOHN LONDON and GEORGE H. TWENEY. *Jack London: A Bibliography.* Georgetown, Calif.: Talisman Press, 1906. Enlarged edition, Millwood, N. Y.: Kraus Reprint Corp., 1973. This monumental work, containing over four thousand entries, lists London's publications, including motion pictures

based upon his works, with reprints and translations, as well as writings about London in English and foreign languages. Professor Woodbridge periodically lists addenda to this bibliography in the *Jack London Newsletter*. Additional bibliographical items are published in *What's New About London, Jack?* (see note 4 in *Chapter Five*).

2. Biography

Of the more than one hundred books and pamphlets published about London, none can be called definitive, but the following are the most significant.

LONDON, CHARMIAN. *The Book of Jack London*. 2 vols. New York: Century, 1921. Sentimental, poorly organized; mostly a pastiche of Jack's own letters, notes, quotes; still the richest source of information about London's life.

LONDON, JOAN. *Jack London and His Times*. New York: Doubleday, 1939. Reissued with a new introduction by the author, Seattle: University of Washington Press, 1968. This carefully written and well-organized biography by London's daughter complements Charmian's work; much of the book relates, however, to the milieu rather than to the man.

STONE, IRVING. *Sailor on Horseback: The Biography of Jack London*. Cambridge, Mass.: Houghton Mifflin, 1938. Though unreliable, this "Biographical Novel," as it was subtitled after reviewers discovered numerous passages plagiarized from London's own writings, has probably done more to popularize London than any other book not written entirely by Jack himself. It has appeared in a score of foreign editions, in Braille, and in more than a dozen paperback reprintings. See Earle Labor, "An Open Letter to Irving Stone," *Jack London Newsletter*, II (September–December, 1969), 114–16, for an indictment of Stone's scholarly deficiencies.

WALKER, FRANKLIN. *Jack London and the Klondike: The Genesis of an American Writer*. San Marino, Calif.: Huntington Library, 1966. Scholarly and articulate—an indispensable guide to London's Northland experience and writings.

3. Criticism

No full-scale critical study of London's writings has appeared in English, but hundreds of articles and reviews have been published. The following list is, of necessity, highly selective; generally, works cited in chapter notes are not repeated here. The Woodbridge and the Walker-Sisson bibliographies may be consulted for more extensive coverage.

BROWN, DEMING. "Jack London and O. Henry." *Soviet Attitudes toward American Writing.* Princeton, N. J.: Princeton University, 1962. Despite London's loss of ideological respectability, he continues as the most popular American writer in Soviet Russia because of his forthrightness, largeness of heart, hardihood, and optimism (*cf.* Bykov, below).

BRUCCOLI, MATTHEW J. "Introduction." *The Sea-Wolf.* Riverside ed. Boston: Houghton Mifflin, 1964. This novel, says Bruccoli, is "perhaps [London's] best," despite the "degeneration of the narrative from meaningful conflict to romance"; ocean functions as moral catalyst. The text established by Bruccoli is definitive.

BYKOV, VIL. "Jack London in the Soviet Union." *The Book Club of California Quarterly News Letter,* XXIV (Summer, 1959), 52–58. Assessment by the leading Jack London scholar in the Soviet Union; says that because of narrative clarity, life-assertive force, and presentation of "noble" man, London's "fiction is more popular in the U.S.S.R. than that of any other foreign author. Although Boris Gilenson, "Hemingway, Our Living Contemporary," *Soviet Life,* CLIV, 7 (July, 1969), 46–47, says that Hemingway is now the most popular foreign writer in the Soviet Union, Bykov, in a letter to the author dated November 23, 1973, reaffirms London's status as the best known and most popular American writer among the common people.

CALDER-MARSHALL, ARTHUR. "Introduction." *The Bodley Head Jack London.* 4 vols. London: The Bodley Head, 1963, 1964, 1965, 1966. Each volume is introduced by a critical essay dealing with the titles in that volume. London is depicted as "the New Twentieth Century Man."

DHONDT, STEVEN T. "Jack London's Satire in *When God Laughs.*" M.A. Thesis. Utah State University, 1967. Treats a neglected but important facet of London's work: his keen sense of irony, as it related to his class consciousness.

———. " 'There Is a Good Time Coming': Jack London's Spirit of Proletarian Revolt." *Jack London Newsletter,* III (January–April, 1970), 25–34. Interprets "A Curious Fragment" as "satire on ignorance" and "The Apostate" as prophecy of proletarian hope in education and spirit of revolt.

HENDRICKS, KING. *Jack London: Master Craftsman of the Short Story.* Logan: Utah State University, 1966. Cites three major characteristics of London's writing: ability to create a narrative, to create an atmosphere, and to use irony; "To Build a Fire," "Love of Life," "The Law of Life," and "The Chinago" discussed as exemplifying these qualities.

LYNN, KENNETH S. "Jack London: the Brain Merchant." *The Dream of Success.* Boston: Little, Brown, 1955. "London's socialism clearly reflects the success aspirations of an ex-newsboy and reveals the impingement of the life outlook of Horatio Alger on that of Karl Marx."

MARTIN, JAY. *Harvests of Change: American Literature, 1865–1914.* Englewood Cliffs, N. J.: Prentice-Hall, 1967, pp. 62, 208, 234–37. London was a "philosophical" rather than a "literary" fictionist; his "very life and mind is a demonstration of the multiplicity of the modern mind that they had predicted."

McCLINTOCK, JAMES I. "Jack London's Short Stories." Ph.D. Diss., Michigan State University, 1968. Intelligent and comprehensive.

––––. "Jack London: Finding the Proper Trend of Literary Art." *The CEA Critic,* XXXIV (May, 1972), 25-28. The magazine debate over Romance vs. Realism shaped London's theory of art.

McMILLAN, MARILYN JOHNSON. "Jack London's Reputation as a Novelist: An Annotated Bibliography." M.A. Thesis. Sacramento State College, 1967. London's contemporaries "were favorable towards the works that were concerned with adventure and romance and hostile towards the philosophical socialism expressed in others."

MILLS, GORDON. "Jack London's Quest for Salvation." *American Quarterly,* VII (Spring, 1955), 3–14. London's work was "in large measure simply an expression of the age-old problem of the unbridled will and the brotherhood of man, but presented in the vocabulary of materialistic thought."

PATTEE, FRED LEWIS. *The Development of the American Short Story.* New York: Harper, 1923, pp. 347–53. Best short critique of London's contribution to this genre.

PETERSON, CLELL T. "The Jack London Legend." *American Book Collector,* IX (April, 1959), 15–22. Significant analysis of the civilization vs. wilderness theme in London's work; concludes that the tension was never resolved but worsened during his last years.

SHIVERS, ALFRED S. "Jack London: Author in Search of a Biographer." *American Book Collector,* XII (March, 1962), 25-27. Points out deficiencies in major biographies and in London's own autobiographical writings.

––––. "Jack London's Mate-Women." *American Book Collector,* XV (October, 1964), 17–21. London's "typical heroine is a varying composite made up of four women in the author's life: Bess Maddern[,] Charmian Kittredge, . . . Mabel Applegarth, [and] Anna Strunsky."

SIMPSON, CLAUDE M., JR. "Jack London: Proletarian or Plutocrat?" *Stanford Today,* Series 1, No. 13 (July, 1965), 2–6. Concludes that "this paradoxical man is neither proletarian nor plutocrat," but the unstable and self-destructive mixture of both.

WALCUTT, CHARLES CHILD. *Jack London.* Minneapolis: University of Minnesota, 1967. An important but hastily written pamphlet.

WALKER, DALE L. *The Alien Worlds of Jack London.* Grand Rapids, Mich.: Wolf House Books, 1973. A pioneering critical survey of London's "fantasy fiction."

WALKER, FRANKLIN. "Afterword." *The Sea-Wolf and Selected Stories.* New York: New American Library, 1964. "Like Conrad, London combined a love of adventure, based largely on personal experience, with an inquiring mind that constantly puzzled over the nature of man and his relation to his environment."

————. "Ideas and Action in Jack London's Fiction." *Essays on American Literature in Honor of Jay B. Hubbell.* Ed. Clarence Gohdes. Durham, N. C.: Duke University, 1967. Fresh, perceptive assessment of London as a folk hero.

————. "Jack London: *Martin Eden.*" *The American Novel from James Fenimore Cooper to William Faulkner.* Ed. Wallace Stegner. New York: Basic Books, 1965. Excellent appreciation of a novel which retains its vital appeal despite its artistic unevenness.

WILCOX, EARL. " 'The Kipling of the Klondike': Naturalism in London's Early Fiction," *Jack London Newsletter,* VI (January–April, 1973), 1–12. In his Northland stories "London asserts the Kiplingesque myth of the superior White Race, but he also adapts it to a naturalistic framework. For the survival thesis is clearly Darwinian in import."

Index

Adams, Henry: *The Education of Henry Adams*, 27-28, 30, 153n
Aeschylus, 67
Alger, Horatio, 149, 170
Almand, William F., Jr., 160n
American Book Collector, 164n
American Dream, The, 8-9, 17-21, 25, 36, 82-102, 121-23, 149, 170
Anderson, Sherwood, 155n
Applegarth, Mabel, 17-18, 22, 44, 151n, 171
Aristotle (theory of tragedy), 63-67, 156n
Atlantic Monthly, 7, 15, 18, 40-41, 47-48, 49, 154n

Bachelard, Gaston, 105
Baird, James: *Ishmael: A Study of the Symbolic Mode in Primitivism*, 60-61, 155n
Bamford, Georgia Loring, 154n
Baskett, Sam S., 152n, 162n, 163n, 164n
Bennett, Arnold, 84
Bergson, Henri, 21
Berton, Pierre, 35, 37, 153n
Bierce, Ambrose, 45, 94, 99
Black Cat (magazine), 44, 47
Blake, William, 8, 92
Blatchford, Winifred, 84, 158n
Blotner, Joseph, 101, 159n
Bonaparte, Princess Marie, 105
Books in Print, 8, 148
Boston American, The, 100
Bowen, James K., 156n
Brett, George P. (President of The Macmillan Company), 71, 78, 84, 91, 136, 157n, 159n, 161n
Bridge, James Howard (Editor of the *Overland Monthly*), 45

Brown, The Reverend Charles, 116
Brown, Deming: *Soviet Attitudes toward American Writing*, 169
Browning, Elizabeth Barrett, 104, 159n
Browning, Robert, 95
Bruccoli, Matthew J., 169
Bubka, Tony, 167
Buck, Philo, Jr., 147, 163n
Bulletin, The (San Francisco), 42-43
Burbank, Luther, 18
Burnham, John C., 160n
Bykov, Vil, 169

Campbell, Joseph: *The Hero with a Thousand Faces*, 77, 157n
Calder-Marshall, Arthur, 169
Carlson, Roy W., 152n, 159-59n
Carroll, Lavon B., 151n
Carroll, Lewis [pseud. Charles Lutwidge Dodgson], 125
Century Illustrated Monthly Magazine, The, 7
Chaillu, Paul du, 23
Chaney, William Henry, 15, 21, 153n
Chase, Richard, 72, 157n
Chateaubriand, François René de, 61
Cirlot, J. E., 157n
Clemens, Samuel Langhorne. *See* Twain, Mark
Collier's, 7, 16
Commager, Henry Steele, 28, 152n, 153n
Conrad, Joseph, 19, 67, 132, 162n, 171
Cooper, James Fenimore, 127, 164n

173

Cosmopolitan, 7, 41, 49, 69, 114, 142
Coxey, "General" Jacob (Coxey's Army), 28, 30
Crane, Stephen, 9, 147
Cravens, Hamilton, 160n
Crèvecœur, Hector St. John, 141

Danvers, Donald, 155n
Darwin, Charles, 32, 153n, 171
Day, A. Grove, 161-62n
Debs, Eugene V., 104
Dhondt, Steven T., 162n, 169
Dickens, Charles, 33
Dreiser, Theodore, 41, 149; *Sister Carrie*, 120-21

Eames, Roscoe, 161n
Edmondson, Elsie, 163n
"Education Novel," 116-22
Edwards, Jonathan, 125
Eliade, Mircea, 59, 108-109, 155n
Eliot, T. S., 87, 96, 127, 147, 152n
Ellis, James, 159n
Emerson, Ralph Waldo, 20, 125
Erbentraut, Edwin B., 162n
Erie County Penitentiary, 31
Everhard, Ernest, 30
Everhard, Mary, 30
Everybody's Magazine, 106

Faulkner, William, 125, 127, 147, 148
Feied, Frederick, 164n
Fish, Robert L., 167
Fitzgerald, F. Scott: *The Great Gatsby*, 82, 122, 148, 149
Foner, Philip, 104, 158n, 159n
France, Anatole, 104
Franklin, Benjamin, 9, 83
Frazer, Sir James George: *The Golden Bough*, 75
Freud, Sigmund, 8, 19, 56-57, 75, 108
Frontier, The, 19-21, 27, 152n
Frost, Robert, 155n

Garland, Hamlin, 36, 153n

Garnett, Porter, 89, 158n
Geismar, Maxwell, 56-57, 72, 75, 104, 105, 113, 154n, 157n, 159n, 160n
Genteel Tradition, 40-42, 98-100, 154n
George, Henry, 117
Ghent, W. J.: *Our Benevolent Feudalism*, 102
Gilenson, Boris, 169
Giles, James R., 157n, 158n
Goddard, Charles, 156n
Goethe, Johann Wolfgang von: *Wilhelm Meister's Apprenticeship*, 117
Gohdes, Clarence, 171
Grey, Zane 149

Haeckel, Ernst, 20
Hardy, Thomas, 41
Harper's, 7, 41
Harvard University, 30, 100
Hatcher, Harlan, 148
Hawaii, 16, 127-31, 161-62n
Hawthorne, Nathaniel, 59
Hearst, William Randolph, 100
Hemingway, Ernest, 9, 41, 132, 147, 148, 150, 162n, 169
Hendricks, King, 46, 147, 151n, 154n, 156n, 163n, 167, 169-70
Henry Clay Debating Society, 32
Heron, Herbert, 167
Henry, O. [pseud. William Sidney Porter], 149
Hicks, Granville, 82, 157n
High School Aegis, The (Oakland Calif.), 15, 32
Hinkle, Beatrice M., 160n
Hoffman, Elwyn, 48, 86, 164n, 158n
Hoffman, Frederick J., 158n
Hopper, James, 33-34
Holland, Robert Belton, 163n
Howells, William Dean, 41, 148
Hudson, William Henry, 62, 141
Huxley, Aldous, *Point Counter Point*, 68

Illustrated Buffalo Express, The, 38

Intercollegiate Socialist Society, 100
Irving, Washington, 23

Jack London Newsletter, 168
James, George Wharton, 80, 157n
James, Henry, 37-38, 86-87, 106, 147, 148
James, William, 18, 40
Jesus, 129
Johns, Cloudesley, 47, 67, 82, 87, 90, 91
Johnson, Martin, 161n
Johnson, Samuel, 84
Johnston, Mary: *To Have and To Hold*, 40-41, 154n
Jones, Howard Mumford, 20, 152n
Joyce, James, 147
Jung, Carl G., 8, 9, 19, 57-59, 67, 78, 79, 121, 127-29, 154n, 155n, 157n, 160n, 161n, 163n
Junior Munsey Magazine, 87

Kant, Immanuel, 33
Kazin, Alfred, 151n
Kelly, "General" Charles T. (Kelly's Army), 30
Kidd, Benjamin, 20, 33, 153n
Kipling, Rudyard, 19, 50, 71, 86, 154n, 171
Klondike gold rush, 15, 17, 35-39, 42-43, 153n
Knapp, Margaret L., 41
Koestler, Arthur: *Darkness at Noon*, 114-15
Kropotkin, Prince Peter, 40
Kruskopf, Anders, 161n

Labor, Earle, 156n, 161n, 164n, 168
Lane, Rose Wilder, 158n
Lawrence, D. H., 117, 121
Lay, Wilfrid, 160n
Lesser, Simon O.: *Fiction and the Unconscious*, 157n
Lewis, Austin, 89
Lewis, R. W. B.: *The American Adam*, 21, 153n
Lewis, Sinclair, 16, 149, 162n
London, Bess (Becky), 15, 145, 171

London, Bessie Maddern, 15, 16, 90-91
London, Charmian Kittredge, 16, 91, 96, 102, 128, 143, 145, 153n, 156n, 157n, 160n, 161n, 163n, 168, 171
London, Eliza, *see* Shepard, Eliza London
London, Flora Wellman, 15, 21
London, Ida, *see* Miller, Ida London
London, Jack (John Griffith): agricultural interests, 8, 18, 143-46; astral projection, 8, 113-15; autobiographical elements in writings, 23-25, 48, 102-103, 115, 116-23, 143-45, 170; birth, 15, 17, 21-22; boxing stories, 9, 142, 164n; death, 7, 16, 18, 122-23, 145, 161n; environmentalism, 70, 79-80, 99, 138, 141, 171; fantasy, 44, 56-57, 101-14, 149, 160n, 171; hoboing, 8, 29-32, 149, 164n; irony and satire, 8-9, 64-67, 88, 132-36, 144, 150, 162, 169; Klondike experiences, 15, 17, 35-39, 42-43; literary theory and professionalism, 20, 31-32, 34-35, 43-44, 83-89, 158n, 170; love and woman, 89-91, 96-100, 102-104, 140-45, 163n, 170-71; magazine sales, 7, 45-47; mythopoeic genius, 9, 43, 49, 57-81, 108-109, 125-26, 157n; Northland code, 50-56, 126, 132, 133; penal reform, 18, 31, 113-14, 149, 160n; philosophy, 9, 31-34, 60-61, 67-68, 80, 90-91, 96, 98, 126, 152-53n, 159n, 170, 171; poetry and poetic elements, 21, 34, 46-47, 72, 74, 87, 89, 104, 151n, 167; race theories, 20, 68, 133-34, 153n, 155n, 156n, 171; ranch, 15, 16, 102, 136-37, 143-45, 163n; reading habits, 22-23, 31-33; *Snark*, 16, 124-26, 131, 161-62n; Socialism, 8, 15, 16, 18, 21, 33, 60, 89, 100-105, 152-53n, 170; style and writing habits, 26,

31-32, 37-38, 40-48, 69, 86-89, 149-50, 169-70; success myth, 7-9, 18, 28-29, 42-49, 115-23, 151n, 170; writing contests, 17-18, 25-26, 151n

WORKS:

Abysmal Brute, The, 16, 137, 142, 162n, 166
Acorn-Planter: A California Forest Play, The, 163n, 166
Adventure, 162n, 166
"All Gold Canyon," 8
"Apostate, The," 23-24, 153n
Assassination Bureau, Ltd., The, 167
"Bâtard," 70-71, 135
Before Adam, 106-109, 110, 113, 160n, 166
"Bones of Kahekili, The," 128
Burning Daylight, 137, 138-42, 149, 162n, 166
Call of the Wild, The, 9, 15, 39, 59, 69-81, 94, 111, 150, 157n, 166
Children of the Frost, 157, 155n, 165
"Chinago, The," 8, 162n, 170
"Chun Ah Chun," 162n
Cruise of the Dazzler, The, 24, 25, 165
Cruise of the Snark, The, 124, 127, 131, 161n, 162n, 166
Daughter of the Snows, A, 15, 67-69, 91, 156n, 162n, 166
Daughters of the Rich, 167
"Dream of Debs, The," 105
Dutch Courage and Other Stories, 167
Faith of Men, The, 166
"First Aid to Rising Authors," 87
"Frisco Kid" stories, 32
From Dawson to the Sea, 39
Game, The, 164n, 166
"Getting into Print," 158n
God of His Fathers, The, 60, 155n, 165
Gold, 167

"Gold Hunters of the North, The," 153n
"Goliah," 105
"Good-by, Jack," 131
Hearts of Three, 69, 156n, 162n, 167
"House Beautiful, The," 158n
House of Pride and Other Tales of Hawaii, The, 161n, 162n, 166
"How I Became a Socialist," 153n
Human Drift, The, 167
"In a Far Country," 50-51, 53-57, 62, 75
"In the Forests of the North," 59
Iron Heel, The, 30, 101-105, 111, 137, 149, 158n, 159n, 160n, 166
"Jack London by Himself," 35
Jerry of the Islands, 137, 162n, 167
John Barleycorn, 16, 29, 34, 37, 42, 45, 48-49, 153n, 166
"Jokers of New Gibbon, The," 133
"'Just Meat,'" 8
Kempton-Wace Letters, The, 90-91, 158n, 166
"Koolau the Leper," 129-31
"Law of Life, The," 8, 150, 170
"League of Old Men, The," 3
Little Lady of the Big House, The, 137, 142-45, 162-63n, 167
"Lost Face," 8
Lost Face, 166
"Love of Life," 8, 170
Love of Life and Other Stories, 166
"Madness of John Harned, The," 164n
Martin Eden, 31, 47, 48, 69, 82, 85, 116-23, 124, 149, 151n, 154n, 158n, 160n, 161n, 166
"Material Side, The," 87, 158n
"Mauki," 134-36
"Mexican, The," 9, 164n
Michael Brother of Jerry, 137, 156n, 162n, 167

"Minions of Midas, The," 105
Moon-Face and Other Stories, 166
Mutiny of the Elsinore, The, 69, 166
"My Hawaiian Aloha," 161n
"Night-Born, The," 9
Night-Born, The, 164n, 166
"Odyssey of the North, An," 15, 47, 50, 154n
On the Makaloa Mat, 129, 161n, 167
"On the Writer's Philosophy of Life," 158n
"Other Animals, The," 16
"Pat and Mike" joke, 46
"Pearls of Parlay, The," 155n
People of the Abyss, 8, 15, 18, 91-94, 149, 158n, 166
"Phenomena of Literary Evolution, The," 158n
"Piece of Steak, A," 9, 164n
"Red One, The," 160n
Red One, The, 167
Revolution and Other Essays, 153n, 154n, 158n, 166
Road, The, 29, 31, 32, 84, 149, 153n, 166
"Samuel," 9
Scarlet Plague, The, 109-13, 160n, 166
Scorn of Women, 166
Sea-Wolf, The, 8, 94-100, 102, 115, 144-45, 150, 159n, 166, 171
"Sheriff of Kona, The," 131
"Shin Bones," 138, 161n
Smoke Bellew, 166
Son of the Sun, A, 132, 133, 155n, 162n, 166
Son of the Wolf, The, 15, 48, 50, 51, 53, 61, 62, 154n, 165
South Sea Tales, 132, 133, 134, 166
Star Rover, The, 106, 113-15, 149, 160n, 166

"Story of a Typhoon off the Coast of Japan," 25-26
"Strength of the Strong, The," 105, 159n
Strength of the Strong, The, 159n, 166
Tales of the Fish Patrol, 25, 166
"Tears of Ah Kim, The," 128
"Terrible and Tragic in Fiction, The," 105, 158n
"Terrible Solomons, The," 131, 162n
Theft, 166
"These Bones Shall Rise Again," 154n, 158n
"Thousand Deaths, A," 44
"To Build a Fire," 59, 63-67, 150, 155-56n, 170
"Told in the Drooling Ward," 8
"To the Man on Trail," 15, 45, 51-53
Turtles of Tasman, The, 167
Valley of the Moon, The, 25, 69, 137, 142, 149, 153n, 162n, 166
"War," 9
War of the Classes, 32, 153n, 159n, 166
"Water Baby, The," 128-29
"What Communities Lose by the Competitive System," 158n
"What Life Means to Me," 82
"When Alice Told Her Soul," 128
When God Laughs and Other Stories, 162n, 164n, 166, 169
"When He Came in" (triolet), 46-47
"Where Boys Are Men," 152n
White Fang, 62, 69-70, 78-81, 94, 137-38, 142, 150, 157n, 162n, 166
"White Silence, The," 45, 61

London, Joan, 15, 21, 94, 103, 113, 145, 153n, 154n, 157n, 158n, 159n, 168
London, John, 15, 22
London, John (bibliographer), 157n
London, Joy, 16

London Collector, The, 164n
Lynn, Kenneth S., 42, 151n, 154n, 170

Macmillan Company, The. See Brett, George P.
McClintock, James I., 161n, 170
McClure's Magazine, 49
McMillan, Marilyn Johnson, 170
Maddern, Bessie. See London, Bessie Maddern
Mailer, Norman, 150, 164n
Malamud, Bernard: The Fixer, 115
Mann, Thomas, 155n
Martin, Jay, 170
Marx, Karl, 20, 33, 60, 102, 117, 153n, 170
Maugham, W. Somerset: Of Human Bondage, 117
Melanesia, 131-36, 137
Melville, Herman, 8, 148; Moby-Dick, 59-62, 95, 121
Miller, Ida London, 15
Mills, Gordon, 95, 159n, 164n, 170
Milton, John, 17, 95
Morrell, Ed., 113-14, 160n
Morning Call (San Francisco), 25-26
Morison, Samuel Eliot, 28, 153n
Muller, Herbert: The Spirit of Tragedy, 67, 156n

Nakata, 16
Naturalism, 69-81, 95-99, 112, 115, 120-21, 131-33, 156n, 159n, 164n, 171
New Criticism, The, 147-48
Nietzsche, Friedrich, 20, 95, 153n
Norris, Frank, 40, 113

Oakland High School, 15, 32
Oakland Public Library, 23
Occident, The, 87
O'Connor, Richard, 154n, 158n
O'Neill, Eugene, 96
Ouida [pseud. Marie Louise de la Ramée], 23

Overland Monthly, 15, 44-45, 47, 48, 51, 53

Pascal, Blaise, 62
Pattee, Fred Lewis, 40, 49, 152n, 170
Pearsall, Robert Brainard, 159n
Peterson, Clell T., 143, 151n, 154n, 156n, 162n, 170
Phelps, Elizabeth Stuart, 41
Phillips, Roland (Editor of Cosmopolitan), 114, 142
Poe, Edgar Allan, 59, 69, 105-106, 109-10, 148
Prentiss, Jenny, 15, 24
Primitivism, 59-81, 99, 110-12, 120-21, 155n, 157n

Quinn, Arthur Hobson, 147, 163n

Realism, 31, 40-42, 85-87, 149-50, 170
Rideout, Walter B., 104, 159-60n
Riis, Jacob, 40
Roberts, Charles G. D.: The Kindred of the Wild, 71-72, 157n
Roosevelt, Theodore, 16, 50
Rothberg, Abraham, 163n
Rousseau, Jean Jacques, 61

Santayana, George, 60
Saturday Evening Post, The, 7, 69, 71
Saunders, Margaret Marshall, 71
Schlottmann, David H., 164n
Seton, Ernest Thompson, 71
Shakespeare, William, 95
Shearer, Floyd, 151n
Shepard, Eliza London, 15
Shepard, Irving, 147, 151n, 153n, 154n, 167
Shepard, J. H., 37
Shivers, Alfred S., 156n, 161n, 170-71
Simpson, Claude M., Jr., 171
Sinclair, Upton, 163n
Sisson, James E., 157n, 159n, 162n, 167, 169

Slocum, Joshua: *Sailing Alone Around the World*, 124
Smith, Adam, 32-33, 117
Smith, Henry Nash: *Virgin Land*, 136
Socialist Labor Party, 33, 100
Sophia Sutherland (sailing schooner), 25
Sophocles, 67
Spencer, Herbert, 33, 60, 86, 102, 117, 153n
Spiller, Robert E., 95, 104, 159n
Springer, Anne Marie, 163n
Stegner, Wallace, 160n
Sterling, George, 94
Stevenson, Robert Louis, 19
Stolz, Herbert, 161n
Stolz, Louis H., 161n
Stone, Irving, 103, 113, 159n, 161n, 168
Stowe, Harriet Beecher, 33
Strunsky, Anna. *See* Walling, Anna Strunsky
Swinburne, Charles Algernon, 119-20

Tarkova, Yelena, 151n
Thoreau, Henry David, 35, 124
Thorsen, W. B., 164n
Tochigi, 161n
Tolstoi, Leo, 41
Town Topics, 46
Trotsky, Leon, 104
Tunney, Gene, 164n
Turner, Frederick Jackson, 27, 152n
Twain, Mark, 19-20, 30, 84, 148, 149; *Adventures of Huckleberry Finn*, 24, 39
Tweney, George H., 157n, 167

University Academy (Alameda, Calif.), 33
University of California (Berkeley), 15, 26, 33-34

Vivas, Eliseo, 81, 157n

Walcutt, Charles Child, 67, 156n, 164n, 171
Walker, Dale L., 167, 169, 171
Walker, Franklin, 19, 116, 147, 152n, 156n, 160n, 162n, 168, 171
Walling, Anna Strunsky, 83, 89-92, 158n
Wecter, Dixon, 17, 19, 151n
Weiderman, Richard, 164n
Weismann, August, 160n
Westbrook, Max, 15, 151n
Weston, Jessie L., 127
What's New About London, Jack?, 164n, 167
Whitman, Walt, 21, 149
Wilcox, Earl, 171
Wilshire, Mary, 160n
Wolfe, Thomas, 117
Woodbridge, Hensley C., 147, 157n, 159n, 164n, 167-68, 169

Yale University, 30, 100, 159n
Yardley, Jonathan, 160n
Young, Philip, 58, 155n
Young, Thomas Daniel, 163n
Youth's Companion, The, 18, 43, 152n

Zirkle, Conway: *Evolution, Marxian Biology, and the Social Scene*, 96, 152n, 159n

8940